aLL the courses in the kingdom

aLL the courses in the kingdom

an american plays
at the birthplace of golf

richard e. peck

REPertory   *Placitas, New Mexico*

REPertory Publishing
Placitas, New Mexico

©2003 by REPertory Publishing
Design: Barbara Jellow

Library of Congress
Control Number: 2002096758

Printed in Korea
9 8 7 6 5 4 3 2 1

The paper used in this publication is acid-free.
It meets the minimum requirements of
American Standard for Information
Sciences—Permanence of Paper for Printed
Library Materials, ANSI Z39.48-1984.

For his understanding and love of golf and its history in Fife,
his willingness to share his knowledge and to open doors,
this book is dedicated with affection and respect to

DAVID DOWIE

sportsman, gentleman, Scot

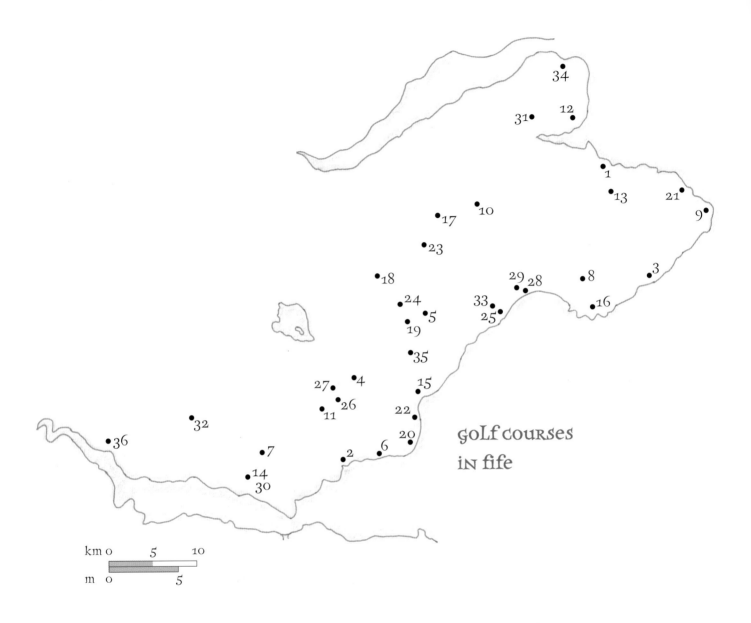

golf courses
in fife

km 0   5   10

m   0   5

contents

acknowledgments

Every book is a collaboration, with thanks owed many for their varied and generous contributions: Individuals like Richard Yarham — who met me at the Edinburgh airport — and his wife Anne, who welcomed me into their home, and Art Bova, for his photographer's discerning eye. Organizations like the Fife Golfing Council, the Kingdom of Fife Tourist Board, and the St. Andrews Links Trust. And individuals so broadly talented that each seems a full organization, like marketing expert, (better-than-average) golfer, accomplished photographer, and raconteur Mike Williamson. Among the many others involved, designer Barbara Jellow deserves special thanks for turning ideas into images and a typescript and scattered photos into the book you're holding. Thank you all.

photo credits

Most photos are by Mike Williamson (MW), taken for the Kingdom of Fife Tourist Board (KFTB). Others are as follows:

Andrew Beveridge: p. 60
Drumoig Golf Club: p. 4
Kingsbarns Golf Club: p. 78
Leemancolour Ltd.: p. 10
Alistair Milne: p. 83
Shona Muirhead: p. 1
Wilson Page: p. 107
Richard E. Peck: cover, pp. viii, 1, 19, 20, 37, 81, 90, 110
MW/KFTB: pp. ii, 12–19, 22–57, 62–80, 86–103, 108, 112–117

*The first hole at Aberdour and the Firth
beyond it.*

preface

The seacoasts of Britain boast the finest links golf courses in the world. The county of Kent in southeast England, for example, is home to Royal Cinque Ports, Prince's, and Royal St. George, a trio of challenging courses ten miles from Dover, near the coastal towns of Deal and Sandwich. Center your vacation in fascinating Canterbury, only eighteen miles away, as my wife and I did a few years ago, and enjoy both the golf and the many flower gardens throughout Kent.

In northwest England, the commuter train rattling north from Liverpool to Southport lumbers along in sight of the Irish Sea. Between the right-of-way and the sea lie five remarkable links courses—West Lancashire, Formby, Southport-and-Ainsdale, Hillside, and Royal Birkdale—one after the other. A few miles farther north, near the tacky carnival glitter of Blackpool, is Royal Lytham and St. Annes, the Open venue as recently as 2001. Back south across the Mersey is Royal Liverpool. All these fine courses are Open or Open-qualifying sites.

Gorse and skellies frame #5 at Anstruther.

Most golfers are familiar with these names, if not necessarily with the courses that they label. The telecast of Sandy Lyle's 1985 Open victory on Royal St. George's crowned, parched fairways revealed to U.S. fans the appearance of the sometimes sunburnt courses in Kent. Those who huddled in the rain-swept grandstands to watch Mark O'Meara's win at Southport's Royal Birkdale in 1998 won't soon forget the dunes and waving grasses, the wind-driven mists and stadium-shaped fairways that mark that marvelous stretch of challenging seaside courses.

But take the trek north through Cumbria into Scotland and the Cheviot Hills, past Edinburgh and across the Firth of Forth into the Kingdom of Fife. The courses peppering this golfing Mecca are paradoxically less well known. Undeservedly so, say golfers who have played them. These courses are where

Town	Area Code	Phone
ANSTRUTHER	1333	311073
BURNTISLAND	1592	872667
CRAIL	1333	450869
CUPAR	1334	652874
DUNFERMLINE	1383	720999
GLENROTHES	1592	754954
KIRKCALDY	1592	267775
LEVEN	1333	429464
ST. ANDREWS	1334	472021

the game has evolved over the centuries to become the addiction so many of us share. Please note that I said "courses," and not simply "The Course."

On several visits to Scotland over the years, like most foreign visitors, I headed straight for Fife and The Old Course at St. Andrews. Each time, I played the Jubilee or New Course as well, other fine venues you'll play while waiting for the daily lottery to give you permission to play The Old Course. After suffering a drubbing there, I dragged my wounded pride to one of golf's other shrines, at Carnoustie, or Troon, or Turnberry. Half the vacation was spent traveling from one "important" course to another rather than golfing. Until a few years ago, like most foreign visitors, I ignored the other 42 courses in Fife, within ten or twenty miles of the Auld Grey Toun.

That itinerary focused on the most famous courses was worth following on the first visit, and perhaps on the second. It's the itinerary that tour operators favor, especially for first-timers visiting Fife. Not to play The Old Course, given the chance, would be unthinkable. Every golfer wants to try the Road Hole, rinse a wedge in Swilcan Burn, or soak a towel in it on the way to the first green, as the St. Andrews caddies do. Picture putting an eighty-footer through the Valley of Sin to commemorate Costantino Rocca's miraculous shot that tied John Daly at the '95 Open. And standing dwarfed in Hell Bunker erases the smugness that it's too easy to feel seeing Jack (or Seve, or Ian, or Nick) on TV, stuck in that same spot.

But after that obligatory foray into history, it's possible to play a number of fine courses whose names don't have the same historical ring. They're near at hand, seldom crowded, and offer the delight of discovery. Spend a week or two day-tripping along the hedge-bordered country roads leading out of St. Andrews and enjoy the other courses in the Kingdom of Fife.

A few years back I started exploring that rich variety of courses, and now I always look forward to sampling them again. I recently visited the links at Elie, Leven, and Crail, and at Lundin shot one of the best rounds of my life. Names like those, however unfamiliar they might be, label courses as challenging as the more famous. Consider Burntisland and Dunfermline and Kingsbarns and Ladybank . . . the list is longer than you'd suspect.

As the twenty-first century begins, there are forty-two courses in the Kingdom of Fife that are *not* The Old Course. More are planned. Several are Open-qualifying courses. A few are council-managed municipal layouts. Many outshine the better-known courses we see celebrated on the Golf Channel. Three-fourths or more are worth a visit, although I don't expect friends on a first trip to Scotland to forgo the challenge of Troon in order to test themselves at Balcomie or even at the marvelous Open-qualifying links course at Leven. Not on their first visit, perhaps, but on their *next* trip . . .

What follows is a tour of all the golf courses in the Kingdom. It starts in St. Andrews, of course, but then goes on to visit twoscore courses only minutes away. It offers a glimpse of a few towns and villages enriched by those courses, and it introduces several Scots whose hospitality makes any visit to Fife's verdant countryside a real delight. Come walk and play the courses with me, or enjoy their rare beauty captured by several talented photographers.

In this county of 504 square miles there is a course for every 8,500 residents. (Compare that to an accessible course for every 31,000 New Yorkers, or 43,000 Californians.) The courses here range from links to upland and parkland. Playing even a handful of them will allow you to recapture the delight of golf where (and how) it was originally played. I've walked them all, and will again.

Come visit all the courses in the Kingdom of Fife.

*Fairway undulations add to the challenges
at Drumoig.*

introduction

"Gawlf" in the United States and "gowf" in Scotland differ in more ways than pronunciation. In the Americas, North and South, golf is a pricey game. In Scotland it's long been a blue-collar sport (even when Mary, Queen of Scots, interrupted her royal duties to sneak off and play a few holes). The Earlsferry Thistle Club, for instance, playing at Elie, only a dozen miles from St. Andrews, was formed in 1875 as an "artisan's club" for carpenters, masons, and firemen. According to the *History of Golf Clubs in Fife*, a richly helpful booklet published by the Fife Golfing Association a decade ago, any "man in Earlsferry who did not play golf, unless for some good and obvious reason, was regarded as something of a crank."

Scots play the game differently as well, in subtle ways. Before heading to Fife, you'll want to work on running pitch shots into the green. Perfect that skill and you can leave two of your wedges at home. Remember that there are few "buggies" in Scotland, so you'll be carrying that golf bag, or towing it, with an umbrella, dry gloves, rain suit, spare towels, clubs, and balls weighing it down. Lighten your load. Scots know better than to fly a lofted shot into a green as resilient as tile. Instead, they'll run a mid-iron from anywhere inside fifty or sixty yards. If one does toss up a high-arching shot it will land a bounce or two short of the putting surface and release to the stick. The backspin that most of us envy in a PGA pro's approach shot is partly a phenomenon of soft Stateside or parkland greens and rarely achieved by amateurs on Fife's links. In most of Britain, in fact, "backspin" is generally considered a tennis term. Adding the long pitch-and-run to your repertoire will bring you two or three strokes a round nearer the unreachable goal of being a complete golfer.

How else do you approach that goal? You stretch your abilities and learn to play amid gorse and heather, in the wind and rain, and on courses less groomed than the immaculate lush carpets of, say, Scottsdale.

Scotspeak

Bents	Variety of grass
Berm	A ridge or shelf
Burn	Small stream or creek
Buggy	Riding golf cart
Featherie	An early handmade golf ball
Fescue	Variety of grass
Gorse	Spiny, thickset shrub
Skellies	Tidal seacoast rocks
Whin	Coarse brush, such as gorse

"Less groomed," by the way, is only a description and not a criticism of Scotland's "natural" courses. Others have been less generous. My desktop calendar quotes Scott Hoch as calling The Old Course "the worst mess I've ever played. I think they had some sheep and goats there that died and they just covered them up." Bobby Jones — who tore up his card and walked off the course on his first visit — Sam Snead, Lee Trevino, and others have also been graphically critical. But in a recent issue of *Senior Golfer*, Lorne Rubenstein reminded us that playing the same flawless, country-club tracks over and over teaches you little. "Get thee overseas," he advises, "and roam around where the game began."

Our courses may be different from the links where the Scots play ("different to," they're likely to say). We also describe the game differently. The claim that Americans and the British are separated by a common language is accurate. I'm not referring to accents, although the sounds of Boston, Dallas, Glasgow, and Liverpool spoken in the same room can make your fillings ache like the screech of fingernails on a blackboard. And BBC announcers' perverse practice of inventing unique pronunciations — like calling Ypres "wipers" — may not provoke controversy (or "con-TRAH-ves-sy"), but it bewilders some Scots as much as it does most Americans, thankyouverymuchindeed.

Even more confusing than differences in pronunciation are the different meanings that Americans and Brits apply to common terms. Asked what a "golf club" is, many Americans will describe their newest graphite-and-titanium or quad-metal Wonderwhacker. Yanks who belong to a golf club will point to the course where they play, and a few may even boast about the building they think of as their "club."

In Scotland, on the other hand, the term "golf club" refers not to a course but to a group of like-minded golfers united by their common affection for the game. They may represent a single profession, village, or even neighborhood. Several of the "golf clubs" in Fife compete on the same course, or set of courses, rather than each club having a separate layout owned by the members. In the town of St. Andrews, for instance, there are at least seven clubs that own no course: the Royal and Ancient, St. Andrews, St. Andrews New, St. Andrews Thistle, and 19th Hole, as well as the sister ladies' clubs of St. Rule and St. Regulus. They play at different times on the different courses in the St. Andrews links complex. They play The Old Course, certainly, but the others as well: New, Jubilee, Eden, and possibly Strathtyrum, but probably not the nine-hole Balgove.

Today there are more than 40 active clubs in Fife. Others have come and gone. Awareness of their distinctive traditions can make a visit to any one of their courses even more interesting. You'll enjoy playing the course at Elie, for example, where the members of at least two separate clubs play today. According to the *History of the Golf Clubs in Fife*, when the Elie Golf House Club and the Earlsferry Thistle Golf Club began play in 1875 over a shared stretch of links land, the layout was little like what we face today.

> The original golfing tract had no specific holes, and the players were free to hit the ball about wherever they wanted! Order eventually prevailed when a six-hole layout was approved, and this was gradually extended as the Club obtained leases of various adjacent tracts of ground. A course of 14 holes was achieved by 1886, and the 18-hole layout, virtually as it is today was completed in October 1895.

There's another admirably un-American practice in the Kingdom. On U.S. courses we tend to pay by the round when playing away from our home clubs. But most Fife courses list greens fees for either a single round or a daily fee for as many holes, or rounds, as you can cram into the day. I've seen golfers playing The Old Course after 10 P.M. A July day this far north stretches to roughly nineteen hours of daylight!

The tradition of affordable golf goes back a long way. The Ladybank Golf Club charged members half a guinea annually — less than $3 U.S. — when the club was formed in 1879. Visitors — termed "strangers" then — paid "exactly what they wished to give and no more." You won't find such bargains today, even in rural Fife, but neither will you have to take out a loan to pay three-figure fees like those at Pebble Beach or Doral or Turnberry.

Each of the clubs in Fife takes pride in its members' golfing achievements — tournaments played and matches won — as well as chronicling donated trophies and medals for which members contend and memorable oddities distinguishing one club's history from another. Burntisland Club members, for instance, can point to a match between James Braid and Harry Vardon — winners of eleven British Opens between them — held at Burntisland on July 15, 1901, though not a witness survives to describe it, and no one even recalls who won. Some other unique achievements commemorated by the clubs include:

- The Four Airs Club once held competitions whose winner took home a "pound of mince or half a pound of sausages."
- One of the first clubs to accept women members, Burntisland, was also among the first to enjoy Sunday golf. Canmore began to host Sunday play in the 1930s, Cupar in 1955 (a clergyman-member resigned in protest), and other clubs followed suit into the 1960s. But Sunday play is still not allowed in the public park we call The Old Course.
- Auchterderran Golf Club members erected fences surrounding the greens on their course to keep grazing cattle off the putting surfaces (so did members at Leslie), and the course greenskeeper removed cowpats from the course every other day as recently as the 1960s. If a ball landed in a cowpat, the clean-and-drop rule applied — not a delight for the fastidious.
- The Kinghorn course, designed by Auld Tom Morris, once boasted three par sixes.
- Visiting Elie, you'll hear a tale of a golf hole named Peggy's in honor of the neighbor lady who confounded greenskeepers by spreading her laundry on the green to bleach-dry in the sun. So they say.

I enjoy tales like these, and even believe some of them, although I also watch for the twinkle in the 50-year-old storyteller's eye when he trots out his hundred-year-old recollections. Invited to have a pint at the nineteenth hole as you're likely to be, you'll get to judge shaggy sheep stories for yourself.

But that's after the round. We're heading to Fife to play golf where the game originated, to play the *courses*, some public, some private but accessible through the *clubs* that developed them. The distinction between courses and clubs, so different from what we expect in the States, is only one of the intriguing characteristics of golf in the Kingdom.

Shortest Courses in Fife

Name	Yards for 18	Type of Course
BALGOVE (ST. ANDREWS)	3,040	Links
ELIE SPORTS CLUB	4,354	Parkland
ANSTRUTHER	4,400	Links
FALKLAND	4,618	Parkland
LESLIE	4,940	Parkland
SCOONIE	4,979	Parkland

Longest Courses in Fife

Name	Yards for 18	Type of Course
THE DUKES	7,271	Parkland
DRUMOIG	7,006	Parkland
JUBILEE (ST. ANDREWS)	6,805	Links
CRAIGHEAD	6,728	Upland
LADYBANK	6,641	Wooded heathland
NEW (ST. ANDREWS)	6,604	Links

The St. Andrew's links complex — all six courses— at the Eden Estuary.

Golfers know that the game began in Scotland, no matter what the Dutch may say about "kolf" or other stick-and-ball games sometimes counted as ancestors of this addiction. But we can narrow the focus. Golf began and developed not in Scotland-as-a-whole, but along the narrow, sandy rim of the Firth of Forth, and more narrowly yet, in the Kingdom of Fife. Most narrowly, in the town of St. Andrews.

Wherever their homes, golfer-pilgrims who make their way to this town at the eastern tip of Fife have played elsewhere on courses modeled after the original here, followed rules first codified here in 1744, used equipment deriving from clubs and balls designed here and formerly — and in the case of hickory-shafted clubs, still — hand-crafted here. And although the goal of their pilgrimage may be playing a single course, a few days spent touring the best courses in the Kingdom can widen their horizons.

Some accidents of history feel inevitable in retrospect. The half-dozen golf courses arranged cheek by jowl at the east end of Fife on the Eden Estuary annually attract hundreds of thousands of single-minded visitors. When golfers first played over the Pilmour links of St. Andrews some 600 years ago, only a madman could have imagined any use for a second course beside the 22-hole layout eventually named The "Old" Course. Now six contiguous courses fill this patch of sandy, windswept soil. Golfers who come to this lovely university and ecclesiastical town intending to play one particular seaside links discover, if they didn't already know, that two other splendid eighteens, the New and Jubilee courses, lie between The Old Course and the broad strip of beach where the racing sequences in *Chariots of Fire* were filmed. Inland from The Old Course are the Eden, Strathtyrum, and Balgove links, all available for public play, all busy nearly every day of the year, and all worth a visit. At the center of them all — and in fact at the center of golf in Fife, in Scotland, and therefore in the entire world of golf — lies The Old Course.

Finishing the round, over Swilcan Burn Bridge, up 18.

the old course

Whatever the great variety of courses available in Fife, play starts here.

More has been written about this stretch of uneven, whin-cluttered, bunker-pitted, maddening and fascinating stretch of links land than any other. The British Open was first played here in 1873 after a dozen years at Prestwick. It moved to St. Andrews because this was the home course of the reigning Open champion, Young Tom Morris. If that principle still applied — playing on the current champion's home course — Aussie Peter Thomson's five Open victories might have moved the tournament Down Under. In 2000 the Open returned to St. Andrews for the 26th time, and the first of however many Open victories Tiger Woods will eventually earn. Since the advent of televised play over The Old Course in the 1950s, its every feature has become familiar to millions who have never set foot on its turf. It's an icon that needs neither description nor praise.

Most golfers have in mind a particular image of the course or some memorable event that took place here. I will never forget watching the final round of the 1970 Open on television and knowing that Doug Sanders would miss the potentially winning 2-foot putt. I knew as well that Jack Nicklaus had more opportunities to win the Open ahead of him, while the final putt over which Sanders hesitated probably represented the only chance he would ever have. I still recall the instant mix of emotions I felt for Sanders: envy for his having reached that moment, and pity for what the next moment was about to bring. Notah Begay's first Open at St. Andrews saw him leading the tournament with a stunning seven under after sixteen . . . until the Road Hole jumped up and bit him, as it would David Duval in his pursuit of Tiger three days later.

Anyone fortunate enough to play The Old Course comes away with a favorite personal story, as well. Finishing my first round over The Old Course several years ago, I crossed Swilcan Burn Bridge with a friend, Chuck Wellborn. Nearly every golfer of note in the history of the game (except for Ben Hogan) has taken that same walk over the modest stone arch, now 800 years old. Standing at the course perimeter on Links Place, just down the street from Rusacks Hotel, were three elderly ladies in black, wearing hats and gloves, on a warmish July day. Without a word, by whatever psychic coincidence Swilcan Burn inspired, Chuck and I reached up and tipped our caps . . . in response to no applause at all but to the memory of crowds' roaring approval that great golfers have earned on the same spot. All three of the ladies — in their own unspoken understanding — smiled, nodded, and silently mimed the applause that our gesture begged.

I've played the course several times since then, and I have read course histories and smiled at the memories others have shared, especially, let me say, Sidney Matthew's *Wry Stories on the Road Hole*. But there's little description or evaluation I could offer that's not already encapsulated in thousands of printed pages and uncountable drawings and photos.

You already know The Old Course.

Open Winners at St. Andrews

Year	Golfer	Score
1873	Tom Kidd	179
1876	Bob Martin	176
1879	J. Anderson	169
1882	B. Ferguson	171
1885	Bob Martin	171
1888	Jack Burns	171
1891	Hugh Kierkcaldy	166
1894	J. H. Taylor	322
1900	J. H. Taylor	309
1905	James Braid	318
1910	James Braid	299
1921	J. Hutchison	296
1927	R. T. Jones	285
1933	D. Shute	292
1939	R. Burton	290
1946	S. Snead	290
1955	P. W. Thomson	281
1957	A. D. Locke	279
1960	K. D. G. Nagle	278
1964	A. D. Lema	279
1970	J. Nicklaus	283
1978	J. Nicklaus	281
1984	S. Ballesteros	276
1990	N. Faldo	270
1995	John Daly	282
2000	Tiger Woods	269

New Course

You may know less about a number of other fine courses near The Old Course — really near. The first tee of the New Course is only twenty paces seaward. More than a century old now, the "New" opened in April 1895 in response to pressure on The Old Course, which it echoes in a number of ways. It flows over the same undulating links land and shows the same pattern of heading out for nine holes, then doubling back on itself. There's a sprawling double green (holes three and fifteen), and the same sea breezes stir the same club-clutching fescue and bents rough.

Where similarities don't exist, players over the years have imagined them, as if "knowing" a course were the same as taming it. The toughest hole on The Old Course is number seventeen, the Road Hole. You'll hear that said of the New Course as well, where number seventeen is a 229-yard par three with a deep bunker on the right, heavy rough on the left. They say that Eden's 432-yard par-four seventeenth is the most difficult on that even newer course.

Unasked, golfers announce, "Most difficult holes? All the seventeens." But Jubilee's 211-yard par-three seventeenth isn't that tough. Strathtyrum's seventeenth is a pussycat: a 326-yard par four, straight away to a big double green. And the nine-hole Balgove course obviously doesn't have a seventeenth. One way to test all the claims you hear — mine included — is to play the courses.

Another commonplace says that Jubilee is the most difficult because the longest. The New Course is counted the best of the lot by some. But if demand is any measure of merit, consider this: only The Old Course requires a lottery system to decide which of the many applicants can play (although the links course at Elie, a dozen miles away, has also resorted to a ballot in the summer).

I'll offer a new claim to consider. The overall quality of play on the New is better than that next door on The Old Course, where once-a-month (or once-a-vacation) golfers and their caddies comprise some of the foursomes . . . or eightsomes. Some visitors play The Old Course only in order to tell their friends at home that they did. Most on the New Course are there to play golf. At 6,604 yards, par seventy-one, it's test enough (and the Jubilee Course is as much tougher as another 200 yards can make it). It may even be "fairer" than The Old Course because of fewer mid-fairway bunkers, fewer blind tee shots, less fairway whin, and greens small enough to putt without using a waist-high backswing.

The first five holes on the New are all potential pars for a weekend golfer,

Broad fairway, clear target, perfect weather . . .
the New Course at its best.

at distances of 336, 367, 511 (par five), 369, and 180 yards. Compare that to Jubilee's opening trio (454 [par four!], 336, and 546 yards) and decide for yourself.

Most golfers enjoy making the turn on the New Course. The ninth hole parallels the Eden Estuary. It's a 225-yard par three . . . with a secret. The putting surface is only partially visible from the tee, an advantage as much as disadvantage because the depressed green is saucer-shaped. Hit the tee shot a little short, a little right, and the slope will take your ball to the pin like gravity pulling water down a drain.

The tenth is tough but fun, calling for a tee shot through an opening between two gorse-cluttered hillsides into a flat landing area of the long (464-yard) par four. Whether you par the hole or not, the exhilaration of seeing your tee shot land safely in play is satisfying. And number eleven, at only 347 yards, rewards a straight tee shot but punishes anything leaked right into the shaggy rough. A fade here will cost a stroke. Or two. Blame the wind.

With fewer spectators to put pressure on your opening tee shot—or to applaud a long, curling putt on eighteen—the New Course is unexpectedly as much fun to play as The Old Course, although friends will show less patience for your recited summary of the round when you get home.

The Eden Estuary whispering beside Jubilee.

juBiLee

Originally twelve holes, and intended to be a ladies' and beginners' course, Jubilee opened on June 22, 1897, in time to celebrate Queen Victoria's Diamond Jubilee. In less than a decade it expanded to eighteen and eventually — after a number of improvements — it became the longest course in the Links Complex, if not the most respected. Commentators make a point of Curtis Strange's dedicating the 1989 opening of the Jubilee not by playing the course but by hitting a single shot off the first tee, since many doubted that it was really ready for play at the time. It's more than ready now.

An extra set of tees — the "Bronze," most forward of four tees — from time to time hosts competitions played with hickories. The Keepers of the Green, for instance, is an organization founded to commemorate the many contributions of Auld Tom Morris to this game, including his original design of Jubilee. Their recent annual Invitational Tournament was played over these links. Each player used five authentic reproductions of the hickory clubs designed, made, and played by Auld Tom 125 years ago.

Longer than the other courses, straighter, and nearer the sea, Jubilee works on you. The more you play it the more interesting it becomes. If The Old Course is quirky and able always to surprise, and often to frustrate, the Jubilee is subtle. We hear the faint rumble of surf for the first time on number three and then fail to notice the sound diminishing as subsequent holes heading east slant away from the water . . . until we come face to face with the estuary beside the eighth tee.

Turning toward home on the back nine leads from one surprise to another. Numbers eleven and twelve are consecutive par fives, one a dog-leg left, the other turning right, then left. The 538-yard twelfth in particular calls for two long shots in the fairway to have any hope of reaching a good position on the deep, narrow, rising green at the end. The narrow, sloping thirteenth green makes for a tough par three. The fourteenth is a long par four to a double green shared with the fourth.

Golfers familiar with the course find themselves anticipating number fifteen. The green is tucked off to the right behind a gorse-covered sand knoll reaching into the fairway. Few of us will hit the perfect tee shot needed to bring the entire green into view; we would need to place the ball nearly 300 yards down the extreme left edge of the fairway (where a hidden bunker lies in wait for the unwary). The second shot is more likely to be partially blind, which will make it all the more satisfying when you launch a mid-iron over the dune and round the "corner" to find your ball lying in birdie range on the small green.

The drive on sixteen demands just as much precision: the shot, not quite blind, must pass through a narrow channel between two mounds. Do you hit it right past the nearer mound onto the widest part of the dogleg fairway and risk reaching the rough? Try to clear the larger hill poking its whin-rich slope into the fairway from the left? Or hit a long draw around that hill? If you play Jubilee enough you'll eventually try all three.

The two closing holes are straightaway but made challenging by bunkers, four around the seventeenth green, five around the eighteenth, and three more that narrow the eighteenth fairway to half its width some 200 yards off the tee. That trio catches a drive or two from every foursome. If one of them is yours, you'll spend time later trying to imagine how to avoid those bunkers, next time . . . and that means Jubilee has caught you. You're already planning to come back.

The new clubhouse for Eden, Strathtyrum and Balgove.

eden

Along with the nine-hole Balgove, the Eden and Strathtyrum courses are inland from The Old Course, at the end of a separate access drive, next to the driving range and the new Links Trust administrative offices. Local attitude toward the courses is illustrated in the course guide that lumps Eden and Strathtyrum in one booklet, while the Old, New, and Jubilee have separate guides. The joint publication implicitly demeans the Eden, a much better course than Strathtyrum.

Eden is more than 1,000 yards longer, for one thing, and more varied. It's a course that would be more celebrated if it were only a few miles farther from its more famous cousins next door. It starts with the shortest par four on the course (326 yards), followed immediately by the longest (449). The course tends to be level, but the fairways are narrow enough to require accurate tee shots in order to score. One jarring artifice is the unlikely pond on numbers fourteen and fifteen. It's not quite in play on either hole and seems a hole dug for decoration rather than a natural hazard.

The Eden opened in 1914, like the New Course in response to the pressure of heavy play on its predecessors. It was intended to be easier than the Old, New, and Jubilee Courses (Strathtyrum and Balgove are easier still).

But the Eden is in a different category. It's the course that hosts several local women's competitions, as well as the Eden Tournament, played every August since 1919. A fair test, frankly easier than the major three, the course is still several notches above Strathtyrum in both difficulty and interest.

strathtyrum

At 5,094 yards long from the medal tees, 4,705 from the front, Strathtyrum is meant to provide ease of play. Designer Donald Steel (who also redesigned and improved the Jubilee and in 1988 tweaked the Eden) had little enough to work with. The holes are short, but each becomes testing at the green. Steel created greens more undulating and tucked behind more obvious mounding than those on the "better" courses he modified. If Strathtyrum has a character it lies in the way it requires players to hit the wedge or short irons stiff in order to score well, even on these short holes. Power off the tee is wasted. Accuracy on the approach counts for more.

Another characteristic distinguishes Strathtyrum from others in the complex: the entire course has only a dozen bunkers, says the course guide. I recall eleven but doubt that I'll return to search for the twelfth. The number of bunkers on the entire course is fewer than the number on the fourth hole alone of The Old Course, or the eighth hole of the New (it boasts sixteen), or the ninth of Eden (eighteen!).

Strathtyrum will reassure rather than challenge.

balgove

And Balgove is easiest of all. Treeless, with scarcely a mound on its level fairways and only a pair of bunkers in sight, it's a par 30: three par fours, six par threes. The course is short and simple, the perfect place to introduce youngsters to the game without their getting in the way of more experienced golfing adults.

So I believed, until I watched two boys about eleven or twelve on the first tee with their father. They patiently re-teed his ball any time the breeze of his whiff or a near miss nudged it off the tee. He lunged and swung off his feet.

An easy stroll on Strathtyrum.

Young golfers starting out.

They congratulated his vigor and looked over their shoulders to see who might be watching. It was clear that they'd have been embarrassed to take him onto one of the other courses in the complex.

To be fair to Balgove, I've also followed an elderly couple with a solid short game, strolling and playing out of one bag despite a rule to the contrary. They seemed pleased with the sunny day, the game, and each other — fine reasons to be on any course.

From one end of the St. Andrews Links Complex to the other, in calm sunshine or wind and rain, golfers are here to enjoy themselves. At this writing there are 37 other courses in Fife, with four more well into the planning stage or already under construction. St. Andrews, where golf began, is where we begin as well, on our way to an alphabetical tour of all the courses in the Kingdom.

2 ABERDOUR

Six miles east of the Forth Road Bridge in Fife, the course at Aberdour — once home to an obliging ball-toting sheep — offers eighteen holes of parkland golf. It's perched above Hawk's Bay on the riverbank north of the islands of Inchcolm, Inchmickey, and Cramond, islands along with a few unnamed rocky piles laid in the Firth like giant stepping stones bridging the way south to Edinburgh. Golf was played near the site in 1897, but the current course — or a nine-hole ancestor of it — opened seven years later and was extended to eighteen holes in 1912. There was an episode a hundred years ago at Aberdour in which a golfer's ball lodged in the wool of a sheep grazing on the course. The sheep ran from the impact and crossed the green. The ball dropped to the putting surface, and the golfer was allowed to play it from there. Locals still tell the story.

The Fife course nearest the city, Aberdour was soon popular with Edinburgh golfers because of proximity and ease of access (a train ticket from the city to the course once cost less than 10p). It offers as well the uncommon combination of a seaside setting and a parkland layout rich with mature trees.

At 5,469 yards, par 67, Aberdour will let you card a respectable score and delight in the splendid views over the Firth throughout the opening nine, if you're not sent packing by the first two holes, a pair of 160-yard par threes. When one is downwind, the other inevitably faces a stiff breeze. Conditions can call for anything from a short iron on one to a fairway wood on the other, with the added challenge of Hawk's Bay lapping at the coast under the flight of the ball. If your natural shot is left to right, take a deep breath and launch the tee shot out over the bay on number two, bringing it back—you can only hope—onto a small plateau green halfway up a steep hillside.

Coming off the second green we follow a path around the curve of Hawk's Bay, its patchy beach and shingle to the left, with Edinburgh stretched out on the shore beyond the Firth. The landing area for the tee shot on three is the

The first green at Aberdour — always in the wind.

most folded and twisted patch of fairway you can imagine. In 1929 — according to Jack Bald's *Aberdour Golf Club, The First Hundred Years* — 600 to 700 tons of sand were excavated from this spot and used to fill bunkers throughout the course. An irregular hole remains, grown over now with grass. The safest shot is one aimed well right toward number four fairway, even at the cost of lengthening the hole a few yards (it's only 307). Try that, or deal with standing as much as three feet above or below your ball in that mid-fairway crater for your second shot.

We turn back east and head for number four green in a stand of trees halfway up the hill, then climb the rest of the way to number five tee. The next five holes traverse a broad slope, and each new vantage is better than the last. Silver Birch, the eighth hole, would improve nearly any course. At 458 yards from the tips, it's a difficult par four made more challenging by a bunker placed to catch the longest tee shot, as well as by a burn crossing the fairway. And it follows the natural curve of the shoreline above a stone wall. Best of all is the view. It's difficult to exaggerate how fine the vistas are out over the islands of the Firth from Aberdour's front nine. Or ten.

Part of the back nine is less impressive. Four of the holes, twelve through fifteen, are crammed into a space only adequate for two. Fairways are narrow, crossing, shared, or contiguous, with no intervening rough. The number twelve green, for example, lies only eight paces from the fourteenth. Bunkers throughout the tight area show little necessary relationship to the greens near them. When you stand on fifteenth tee, anyone in the bunker behind the twelfth green is at risk if your tee shot leaks right. Finish putting fifteen and you walk back toward the fifteenth tee to reach the sixteenth tee box, off to the right. The two fairways cross.

Once past that cramped patch the course opens up again. Number sixteen stretches out to a slight dogleg left, 449-yard par four (382 yards for members), made interesting by a large tree at the corner of the dogleg. The seventeenth is a 350-yard par four and the eighteenth a 190-yard par three, an ending as uncommon as the two par threes that begin Aberdour.

The front nine is worth a trip from wherever in Fife you happen to be. A friend says, "It should have stayed nine holes." But the nine he likes at Aberdour weren't all a part of the original front nine on this site. The fact is, Aberdour has a number of fine holes, the opening pair especially. They're unique not only in Fife, but also among courses anywhere.

And a drink in the clubhouse after the round offers a matchless view, Edinburgh across the shimmering Firth and below the window, seals sunning themselves on the rocks.

3 ANSTRUTHER

A bit of trivia to haul out at the nineteenth hole: The Old Course was once played over twenty-two holes (eleven greens, each played from both sides). It was later shortened to eighteen (or nine greens) when two greens were eliminated. And the R&A clubhouse, opened in 1854, stands on part of the original first and eighteenth fairway. A nineteenth-century map shows essentially today's layout. The "standard" eighteen-hole length thus established is followed worldwide, although less rigidly in Fife than elsewhere. Today a quarter of the courses in Fife, down from nearly half of them at the end of the nineteenth century, are nine-hole layouts.

Anstruther is one of them. Some of the Fife courses host clubs that might like to see the track they play expanded to eighteen, if adjacent land were to become available. Others — like Cupar, perhaps the oldest nine-hole course in Britain — are more than content to be what Americans might term "half-a-course." They take pride in the distinction.

Anstruther is one such course, although some members — like Jimmy Pearson, recently retired after twenty-six years as Anstruther's greenskeeper — wouldn't mind seeing it expand to eighteen. Old-timers still call the course "Billowness," after its splendid seaside location. ("Ness" in Scotland means "mouth," as in Inverness, the mouth of the river Inver. "Billowness" probably describes the tiny rock-littered inlet where the Firth's billows meet the shore.) But whether it is named for the town where it's located or its position embracing waves off the Firth of Forth, Anstruther/Billowness reached its current nine-hole length only relatively lately. Its original ancestor was a five-hole layout inland, replaced in 1891 with a seven-hole course (later extended to nine) at its present location. The course, says the score card, plays to a par of 62, at 4,144 meters (4,532 yards), but that's twice around: 31 for the "front" nine, 31 for the same nine played again as the "back."

Stories about the tradition of hospitality at "Anst'er" aren't exaggerated. My

Anstruther's tower, a tribute to the village war dead.

letter asking about the history of the course reached Sheila Taylor, steward of the Anstruther Golf Club. The centenary booklet published in 1990 is out of print, but Ms. Taylor mailed me her personal copy, along with the plea that I return it on my next visit. When I did, she introduced me to Jimmy Pearson. Over coffee in the snug seaside clubhouse, he described course changes in recent years. Not long ago, for example, the current number two hole, with its green-side tower commemorating the Anstruther war dead, was played as number eight. And during World War II an unlikely vegetable garden clung sidehill to the broad, steep slope that's now a fairway shared by one and nine.

"Broad slope" is the term that comes to mind as you stand on the first tee and drive toward the striped black-and-white pole in mid-fairway atop the hill, positioned to guide this blind opening tee shot. You'll substitute "steep" for "broad" as you trudge up the incline to reach your ball. Not many golfers, amateur or professional, will put their tee shot over the brow of the hill, a good fifty feet above the tee on this deceptive 288-yard hole. The best drive still leaves you unable to see the green (or even the flag), waiting somewhere more than a wedge away. Choosing the right club for the blind second shot will be easier after you've played the hole a time or two. I was lucky enough to join Australian golf writer Bernie McGuire on the first tee and ride his coattails. Our drives lay side by side. He has the better swing, so after he hit a wedge, I punched a nine. We lumbered up over the crest to learn that we'd both been right, or lucky.

While you catch your breath at the top of the hill, be sure to look left across the Firth of Forth, where the links at North Berwick stretch along the south shore of the Firth. In front of you lie Anstruther's two, three, and four laid out west, east, and west along the top of the plateau. All are straightaway holes of no particular distinction, but the variable winds sweeping this hilltop can make a challenge of any of them.

And then there's number five, named "Rockies." At 239 yards, two yards shorter than the par-three ninth, it's also a par three on the card, but experience suggests playing it as a four. The fairway clings halfway down the cliffside to the left, curling around to a tiny green tilted right-to-left steeply enough that even a perfect fade into it may not hold the slick putting surface. Only the supremely self-confident will try driving this hole. Pride under momentary control, I left the driver in the bag and imitated McGuire's laid-up tee shot. My five-iron reached the narrow landing area — perhaps twenty yards wide — a shelf overhanging the seaweed-covered rocks (Scots call them "skellies") poking above the water at low tide out in the Firth below. That left a half-wedge into — and bouncing over — a green that might have been brick. "Rockies" is a testing hole you might hope to par but will finally be pleased to bogey.

Number six is a par three with a shallow, humped green, easy enough. It's the perfect place to take several deep breaths in preparation for the climb back up to the plateau, where the seventh green awaits. That green lies just beyond a second striped pole announcing yet another blind tee shot. The eighth is a straightaway par four, rewarding mainly for the view of the town on display beyond the green, with its scores of moss-tinged gray slate roofs bristling with clay chimney pots. Number nine takes us back down the hill through the site of that former World War II vegetable garden to the clubhouse.

Hardest Courses to Walk

ANSTRUTHER
BURNTISLAND
CUPAR
GLENROTHES
KINGHORN
KIRKCALDY
PITREAVIE
SALINE

Like the rest of the course, the closing hole — a downhill par three — looks easy. But downhill or not, it's 241 yards, and we faced a wind McGuire estimated at twenty to thirty knots. My best tee shot of the day left me twenty-five yards short of the putting surface.

No matter how easy Anstruther looks on paper, you won't card much of a score on it until you've figured out the wind and managed to decipher the subtleties of holes like "Rockies." All in all, it's worth a visit for the views and two or three challenging holes. Your best bet is to go around twice. Learn the course the first time, record your score the second . . . and then stop in the clubhouse for a glass of whatever will help you recover from the four steep climbs from sea level to the top of the plateau. Sheila Taylor will know what to pour.

4 auchterderran

This nine-hole municipal course is located on the edge of the former mining village of Cardenden. On one side lie the small homes of a quiet village, these days likely to serve as a bedroom community for people who work in nearby Kirkcaldy or even across the Firth of Forth in Edinburgh. On the other side of the course are fields planted with crops, and pastures dotted with grazing sheep. Except for the occasional jet taking off from Edinburgh airport and drawing its contrail across the sky, the scene probably hasn't changed a great deal since the course opened in 1904.

The starter spends quiet afternoons seated in his car parked beside the pro shop, watching play on the course. In the window of the shop is a card listing annual membership fees for the municipal courses administered by the Kirkcaldy District Council Department of Leisure and Recreation: six courses, with Auchterderran charging much the lowest fees. It's seldom if ever crowded. When I first visited Auchterderran, the starter said there were only two foursomes out on the course. We talked and watched three boys about twelve years old finishing their round. On a recent Sunday I saw a dozen golfers walking the whin-lined fairways.

There are six fours, three threes, on this course of 5,250 yards (that's twice around) and par 66. The course is basic; bunkers are gouged in the fairway without a raised lip to indicate which side might be the "front" of the bunker, if that matters. Play on the rough fairways is easy enough, but a shot pulled or pushed into the head-high brush at both sides is gone. There is no middle ground. And greens tend to be flat circles simply mowed tighter than the fairways.

A series of literal terms name most greens: Burn, Dyke, Hill, Pond, Ditch, and so on. Number five is a puzzle. Named "Burma Road," it's a 248-yard par three, which is puzzle enough. But to characterize it on the scorecard as the thirteen-stroke index hole (thirteenth out of nine?) — easier, for instance, than the 287-yard par-four seventh — invites bewilderment. Or an argument.

The municpal course at Auchterderran.

The millpond beside the course names one hole. But the celebration of the course surroundings — sheep, pond, fields, houses — rather than the traits of the course itself suggests that those surroundings are more interesting than the course we play.

It's not worth driving very far to visit Auchterderran. The course is adequate to its purpose, but no more than that. The three boys on number nine illustrated that purpose. Each of them flew his second or third shot toward the flag on the 345-yard ninth, landing the ball two bounces short of the green. Each ball rolled to a stop within ten feet of the flagstick. Two of the three boys one-putted, laughing and teasing each other as they played.

No one would rank the course high on a list of the forty-three available for play in Fife. But it's good to be reminded that golf is a game — a game that's supposed to be fun, regardless of the condition of the course, or the cost of membership, or the quality of the competition. Cardenden is fortunate to have an affordable municipal course, named Auchterderran, on which to learn the game.

5   BALBIRNIE PARK

The Markinch Golf Club's former course was damaged during World War II when it served as the site for an artillery emplacement. After the war it closed. The Glenrothes Development Corporation bought the Balbirnie estate and built a new resort course on which former Markinch members play today.

The entrance to the grounds is reminiscent of resorts everywhere: a grand gate and a winding fifteen mph drive through lawns and gardens (over more speed bumps than your rental car can enjoy) and past the former Balbirnie residence. The residence is now a gabled stone hotel in the center of this 400-acre estate. Beyond the hotel, in a wooded area tucked against the base of the hill beside a fast-running burn, stand a new clubhouse and pro shop for the former Markinch club, renamed (in appreciation for the splendid course they've played since 1984) the Balbirnie Park Golf Club.

The course plays through a forest. Where nature hasn't provided thick groves the developer has; there are hundreds of recently planted trees. Among Fife's newer courses and courses newly expanded, Balbirnie Park is one of nine laid out in a double loop, with a stop at the clubhouse possible between nines.

The two nines here differ. The front plays along the ridges over broad fairways, usually in the wind. Use the driver and fire away. The homebound nine (except for numbers ten and eighteen) wend through valleys and cleared aisles between stands of sycamore and evergreen. The fairways are less breezy but tighter, requiring more precise tee shots. At least two of the par fours (numbers twelve and thirteen) are so tight that discretion calls for an iron off the tee.

There are five sets of tee markers at every hole and a number of fine touches throughout the course. Behind the first tree box is a putting green and an area for chipping or working in the two sand bunkers. Early at the first tee? Use the time to warm up your short game.

Outward-bound on Balbirnie Park #10.

The long holes on the front nine are number six, a 478-yard par five, and number eight, a 422-yard par four headed the opposite way. One plays downwind, one up. Be happy with a total of ten for the pair, a par-and-a-half each. They sandwich between them a handsome downhill 200-yard par three that falls away on all sides of the green. It's an easy par after a perfect tee shot. Otherwise . . .

Balbirnie Park is characterized by a surprising number of blind or semi-blind shots—surprising for a modern course, at least. On seven holes the landing area can't be seen from the tee box, not a problem after playing the course a time or two, but it can lead to your visiting unseen bunkers the first time here. More interesting, we fire into ten or more greens—several elevated, others tucked behind a knoll or mound — where the flag is visible, but not the full putting surface. That problem is minimized by the use of markers on the flagstick. A colored ball is placed low, center, or high on the stick, an aid that's common enough in the states but rare in Fife, where it's shared only by Pitreavie.

The printed course guide available in the pro shop is a must for your first round at Balbirnie Park. Buy it, believe it, use it! About number eighteen the guide advises, "Those laying up should LAY UP! Stay well short of the burn — it's all downhill." Trust the advice. After twice following a good tee shot on eighteen by dunking my second shot in the burn — with a four-wood once, a three-iron the next time — I've decided to play the 482-yard par five with driver, five-iron. Fishing my ball from the burn has lost its charm. As a course Balbirnie Park hasn't, and isn't likely to.

6 Burntisland

The intriguingly named "Burntisland" course, playing over terrain once called Dodhead Farm, hosts one of the ten clubs in Scotland continuously active since the 1800s, and the history of the course — detailed in a centennial booklet published by the club — offers a roster of names central to Scottish golf. Open champion, St. Andrews greenskeeper, and course designer Auld Tom Morris surveyed the proposed location and declared it an ideal site, "because the nature of the ground is nice and wavy, which makes it all the more suitable for golf." Willie Park, Jr., of Musselburgh, designed the course in 1892. Thirty years later some holes were modified under the direction of James Braid. In 1986, John Salvesen, former R&A captain and designer of the new Fife courses at Charleton and Elmwood, among others, suggested improvements. Add the name Allan Robertson to the list and you'll find few courses in the Kingdom that haven't benefited from the touch of one of these five.

Golf had been played in Burntisland on links land beside the Firth since 1668 or earlier. The move to higher ground was forced by crowding and increased play on the original lower site and the loss of some land to the encroachment of the railway along the water. Now Burntisland is an upland course with the feel of links about it. Geologists say that a sandy part of the course plays over what amounts to a raised beach, distinguished by fine beach grass called "bents," which is now 200 feet above its original site after an ancient upheaval. The feel of antiquity permeates the course. Recently built courses may imitate the originals, right down to hand-stacked stone walls at the course perimeter. But the rough stone walls at Burntisland are figuratively smoothed by generations of moss and lichen filling chinks between the stones. Walls marking the loop of holes ten, eleven, and twelve are especially moss-soft with age.

The first impression golfers experience arriving at any new course can last well into the round. Skiers driving up the narrow valley to the Taos, New

Downhill to Burntisland's fine clubhouse.

Mexico, ski slopes confront "Al's Run" as their first view — a steep expert slope soaring up like a wall in front of them. Some of the faint-hearted turn tail at the sight and head home. At the top of the ski lift but unseen from the road lie more manageable slopes.

The first fairway at Burntisland can look just as threatening to a first-timer. The narrow uphill fairway slopes steeply right to left away from three evenly spaced bunkers (along the right) and toward out of bounds (on the left). No practice swing allowed on the tee. Hit it cold. Then climb after it and hit a blind shot into a hidden green.

Play doesn't get much easier. Throughout the course, fairways fall off to the left, where out of bounds awaits. I've seen a putt roll slowly off number eight green, pick up speed, and come to a stop forty yards down the steep hill. An approach shot missing that green left may be gone for good. As the course guide advises, leave your hook at home. Burntisland may be short — 5,865 yards, par 70 — but plays longer because of marked changes in elevation and the deep rough.

The tee box at number three introduces a novelty. The front third of a lap-strake wooden longboat stands bow-up with a plank seat stretching from side to side under the bow — a rain shelter. (Its mate, I'd guess the stern third of the same boat, offers similar shelter between the eighth and twelfth tees.) Some 210 yards ahead, number three green is square, a shape not commonly found on modern courses. It fits snugly into the corner of the course, with out of bounds both left — a tall hedge — and beyond the green, at a stone wall.

The Pond and Inchkeith, holes number five and six, are consecutive par threes that take us uphill through natural whin and rough not added to the course but part of the landscape that preceded it. From this new height we enjoy superb views of Inchkeith Island, with its towering lighthouse in mid-Firth, and Edinburgh beyond it. The view from number thirteen may be wider; but this unexpected first sight of the distant horizon is the more dramatic because surprising.

In fact, numbers twelve, thirteen, and fourteen perch atop the highest plateau of the course and offer thirty-five minutes of delight. You may find yourself unconsciously slowing play to enjoy the panorama to the south.

The biggest surprise on the back nine is number seventeen, the most pleasant of the closing holes. At 120 yards, the seventeenth should be easy, but it's a blind shot uphill to a par three, with a barbershop-striped aiming pole as guide. Left of the hidden green, at the bottom of a railroad-tie staircase, lurks a sand bunker eight feet deep, ready to seize any shot short, or long, or left of the pin. Stay right of the aiming pole!

If you pass this test, your reward lies in playing the 315-yard downhill finishing par four. Some golfers will drive it. If not, it's a short pitch to a level green and the likelihood of a birdie to close out the round. An eagle's not impossible.

The charm of Burntisland is difficult to overstate, and difficult to explain. A few holes on the back nine seem relatively easy . . . on a calm day. The greens are true and fair. Restrain the impulse to whale away with the driver. Hit short but straight. Keep the ball in play. When in doubt, stay right. At the finish you'll be surprised — even disappointed — that the round is over, one of the best measures of a course. You'd like it go on.

One mystery remains — the name "Burntisland." Three club members I asked about the town's name couldn't explain. A trip to the library might turn up the answer, but instead I'll offer the inference drawn and shared with me by the course starter at Kinghorn, a few miles east. No island burned here, he said. An old map shows the land adjacent to the original links labeled "Bruntie's Land." Did that become "Burntisland" via a misunderstanding or misspelling?

Maybe. It's a good story. Probably more memorable than the truth.

And Burntisland is a memorable course, full of interest and variety, even for those who know links courses well.

7 CANMORE

Courses in Fife are sometimes known best by the name of the club whose members play over them. Other times they are nicknamed according to an address or location. The town of Dunfermline, in the west of Fife near the M90 heading north from Edinburgh, is home to three such: Canmore (or "Venturefair," situated on Venturefair Avenue), Dunfermline (or "Pitferrane," located in the so-named suburb), and Pitreavie. You can't mistake one for the others after playing them and enjoying a meal or a drink in the clubhouse . . . or on the course. A Canmore member warmed our chilly threesome with a tot of single malt from his flask at the turn.

Canmore is comfortable, the course — at first glance — as hospitable as its members. But the stretch of holes members call "the Amen Corner" can surprise the unwary. Members say the "corner" is comprised of holes ten through thirteen. A visitor to Canmore might add nine to that list. In the midst of this 5,376-yard layout, playing to par 67, a stretch of four or five greatly varied holes lies in wait for any newcomer.

We start on "Centenary" (Canmore celebrated its 100th birthday in 1997). In retrospect, this 257-yard first hole should serve as a warning. It's short. The card says so, and your perception agrees, given the white-sand expanse of a bunker as big as a bus looming in the fairway. Though you'll be tempted to focus on simply carrying the bunker, notice that all that sand is fifty yards short of the green. Clearing the bunker isn't the goal; reaching the green is. Check the club in your hand. The hole calls for more than that.

The next five holes are straightforward enough. Four of them hemstitch their way across the face of a slope that is nearly imperceptible . . . until you realize that you haven't had a level stance yet. Number seven is 143 yards downhill to a plateau green rising from the hillside, tilted up to catch the tee shot. Miss either side of the green and you'll roll another fifty yards, then play back up the hill to a putting surface you can't see. Members John O'Shea and

The depressed green at the center of Canmore's "Amen Corner."

Frank Logan — a pair of Irish-named Scots and my playing companions that day — swore it was an easy par three. They scored a four and a five.

The eighth takes us across a deep valley and up over the crest of a hill to a depressed green marked by a bull's-eye target posted high atop a pole behind it. The next, named "The Loch," leads toward and past a dam on the left and a broad burn running diagonally across the fairway. The burn is hidden beyond the crest of the hill. None of us reached it with our drives, but some do. Both holes will get your attention. "Respect" might be a better term.

Everyone perks up at number ten. The green is invisible from the tee, at the end of the narrowest fairway on the course. It's a 375-yard curving dogleg left, pinched between a hillside on the right and a burn clogged with the snarl of tangled wild hawthorn on the left, out of bounds. Canmore's Amen Corner starts with this par four. The best plan is to play the hole like a true dogleg. The tee shot will bounce left off the slope, so aim well right, almost atop the hill, or when your ball kicks left — and it will — you'll earn hawthorn scratches searching the thorny burn.

The next is the most interesting hole at Canmore. "Quarry" is 374 yards long and 80 feet deep at the far end. You'll need 230 to 240 off the tee, right of center, if you hope to hit a short iron to the green concealed deep in the valley ahead. Left of the green is marshy out of bounds. Right of the green, on the gorse-dotted slope sliding down into the ravine, is the best-placed bunker on the course—five feet wide, thirty feet long, situated to keep clever golfers from shooting into the hillside and letting the ball trickle left down to the putting surface. No shortcuts here. Fly your ball to the pin you can't see. And once you putt out, look around. You might as well be on a one-hole course, surrounded by shaggy hillsides and marsh. The hole was not so much designed as discovered and revealed here, like some of Royal Birkdale's seemingly isolated greens.

We're not out of Amen Corner yet. Number twelve is a 195-yard par three whose putting surface is above us, and 180 yards of that distance is all carry over a deep valley. The next hole is "only" 188 yards, but it requires a blind shot to a canted green with out of bounds on the left and danger to the right, where the slope falls off toward the brush-choked burn we thought we'd finished with on ten.

Count the strokes: two fours, two threes, a total par of fourteen, but par is pretty ambitious. Finishing these four difficult holes two over would be success enough.

With Amen Corner behind us, the rest of the course feels easy . . . until we climb eighteen, named "Up the Hill" for good reason. The three of us agreed — when we stopped halfway up eighteen to take a rest none of us admitted to needing — that all closing holes should be short fives, downhill, leading to birdies and the bar.

In the clubhouse over lunch we skimmed through Charles Stuart's handsome history, *Canmore Golf Club, The First 100 Years*. It's a thorough, affectionate record of course changes, the club members, trophies won, matches lost, and the social as well as sporting pleasures of membership at Canmore. Stuart's book illustrates the camaraderie that marks this club, where visitors are invited to share in the members' pleasure. There's no more welcoming club in the Kingdom.

After listening to comments from several Fife golfers, I was prepared to ignore or even disdain the Charleton course, a commercial venture located on part of the thousand-acre Bonde estate not far from Colinsburgh. The developers describe it as "pay as you play." This term itself puts off some members of Fife clubs and courses, even those whose clubs quietly offer a similar option without advertising the fact. I've played those private tracks with members but have just as frequently walked unannounced into a pro shop or starter's shed and paid to play. What, then, distinguishes Charleton from other courses? It may be the lack of tradition or the absence of a proud membership, though the latter is changing. Charleton is now inviting applications for membership. The course itself is more than inviting.

Charleton opened for play in May 1994. In addition to the par-72, 6,132-yard course, it has a pitch-and-putt course, a driving range, and — rare in Fife — riding carts. If you're tired of the challenge of lugging a set of clubs in Fife's seaside winds, you may want to strap your bag onto a "buggy" and ride a round.

The course feels American, although it was designed by former R&A captain John Salvesen, with a hand from Sir Michael Bonallack. The fairways are wide and level, but the putting surfaces are not. They may be the most undulating single greens in Fife ("single" here eliminates from the comparison the double greens at St. Andrews, Crail, and elsewhere). So while you'll avoid trouble off the tee on most holes, your card may be blemished by more three-putts than usual.

The opening hole is broad and nondescript, but the second starts to make the visit here more interesting. It's a slight left-to-right dogleg, the lush fairway falling off to the right; left out of bounds is pastureland leading to a sycamore grove. On my first visit I counted five pairs of grouse feeding there and saw a red fox curled in on himself against the trunk of a fallen tree.

The new clubhouse on Fife's most "American" course — including riding buggies!

Buzzards nest nearby, as do partridge and a notorious woodpecker whose staccato drumming on a hollow tree can surprise you in mid-backswing any time.

A pair of par fives — numbers four and six, one uphill, one down — sandwich between them a delicate par three. Only 120 yards long, it ends at a green that might have been modeled on a pair of gumdrops, one next to the other. Pin placement is everything here and can vary from a receptive spot in the center to tougher positions atop either of the mounds.

Number eight is an intriguing par three of 177 yards requiring a near-perfect tee shot. The green slopes left to right where the hillside falls off into a burn, so a shot into the right half of the green is gone. Mounds on the left prevent a ball missing the green from trickling onto the putting surface. You won't hit this green except by careful design. Place your ball on the left side of the green and face a downhill putt, or accept the four you'll be lucky to earn.

Two holes on the back nine feature a burn and stone wall crossing the fairway. The tougher one is seventeen, where the shallow green lies pinched between the wall and a hidden bunker. It calls for a precise second shot. Hit your approach a few yards short or long and you'll know why the hole's called "Ha Ha." The other is number thirteen, longest on the course at 557 yards, and the most striking. In addition to the burn at mid-hole, it features a small sycamore grove encroaching on the fairway from the right and a huge Wellingtonia looming beside the green to give the hole its name. This firlike evergreen is more than seven or eight feet across at the base and may well have stood here when golf was a novelty in the Kingdom. The course steward didn't know how many years it took a tree to grow to that size, but he reckoned "it's not much change from two hundred fifty." Whatever its age, a tree that grand deserves having the hole named for it.

As handsome as Charleton is, it's more than the natural setting that invites us back. The course is enjoyable, in spite of the difficult greens. They defeated me on that first visit, and the second, but we have a rematch coming.

9   CRAIL

Balcomie Links

A dozen miles from St. Andrews, at the very tip of Fife's East Neuk, on a wind-raked point of land sweeping down to the North Sea, are two very different courses reached by a narrow lane leading through the town of Crail. One, Balcomie Links, is a traditional course, laid out by Auld Tom Morris a century ago, more than fifty years after play had begun over its eight-hole predecessor on the site. The other, Craighead, is new, designed by Pennsylvanian Gil Hanse and opened for play in June 1998. Both operate out of the same pro shop. Both are championship quality courses in different ways. And both reward a visit, although you won't mistake them for twins, or even cousins.

Four of the first five holes on Balcomie Links play along the seashore, the grumbling waves constantly gnawing at the out-of-bounds beach on the right. The holes range uphill and down and are made challenging by rolling, twisted terrain and uneven lies. Always on the golfer's mind, and often in his face, is the wind, a constant presence. One reward for your visit: the sea is visible from every hole.

If you're long enough to reach the 493-yard number two in two strokes, you'll climb a knoll and delight to find the ball waiting on the green tucked behind it. All of us can enjoy the same thrill on number three, a 178-yard par three. From the tee the flag is visible behind a knobby berm fronting the green, although the base of the flagstick isn't. Your walk after a well-struck tee shot is all anticipation, and finding the ball on the green is your reward. Hell's Hole, the 450-yard par-four fifth, then tests your ego: how much of the dogleg can you cut off with a drive over the sea where it nips into the fairway from the right?

Number eight is another long par four, different from the rest by ending at the only double green on the course, shared with number eleven. You near the

Low tide beside 14 on Balcomie Links.

end of the front nine with an uncommonly low score on the card. No wonder. From the member's teebox (not the longer medal tees) the front nine is only 2,841 yards long, seven fours and a pair of threes, for a thirty-four outbound.

The back nine is even shorter: 2,612 yards long, four threes, four fours, and a five, for 33. Playing the medal tees stretches a long four to a five on each side, making par 69. We play Balcomie at 67, yet no one I've spoken to wants the course longer. Interest lies in the variety of holes and the frequent changes in direction. Except for the two longest holes — number eleven, called "Lang Whang," 496 yards uphill, and the downhill twelve, "The Burn," 528 yards in length — no two are parallel. Your first time on the course will have you keeping an eye on the players ahead of you simply for guidance.

One point of reference is the only stand of trees on Balcomie Links, a small copse of wind-twisted hawthorn left of number ten, then, as you turn back at the next tee, left of eleven. There's a single hawthorn in the rough between eleven and twelve as well.

Three of the par threes are longer than 200 yards, and two call for tee shots like the one back on number three; the flags are visible snapping in the breeze, but the putting surfaces are hidden high above atop the rough-shaggy hillsides. The real beauty is number fourteen, far below the tee box with the sea beside and behind a green canted to catch your tee shot, and the whole of the front nine arrayed beyond it. Only 140 yards away from the tee, the green seems nearly that far below your feet as well. To see the best-struck ball ride the offshore winds and drop curving toward the flagstick is delight enough to bring you back to Balcomie Links.

And the last four holes still lie ahead. To reach them requires walking two or three hundred yards around a point of land on a coastal path damp with sea spray, while high above on your right is the Crail Golfing Society clubhouse, with diners watching from the window-side tables. It's a shock to round the point and find yourself facing a small, sheltered meadow and the 260-yard par-four fifteenth, an easy hole, your reward for getting this far.

The only difficulty ahead is the climb to the car park atop the point at the end of the round. After walking eighteen holes in the wind it seems unfair that you have to face that hill, but the climb is made more pleasant by a sight not really part of the course. A low stone cottage sits beside that curving ascent on a swath of privately owned land wedged in between the Balcomie and Craighead courses. The resident of that cottage — a professor of literature, say grounds crewmen — has tucked a rich, bright flowerbed into his sheltered front garden behind a low stone wall. Daffodils, bluebells, pansies, poppies, sedum, English ivy, miniature blossoms of a dozen kinds, and the spreading foliage of a dozen more variously shaded ground covers offer the perfect excuse to interrupt your climb for a deep breath or two. You might even stand and total your card, an excuse to enjoy the garden.

craighead

The Craighead course at Crail opened in June 1998, a year after its completion — a year to roll and mow and mature the greens. At 6,250 yards (6,728 from the tips) it's 800 yards longer than Balcomie Links, though from the forward tees it's only 150 yards longer than the older track. Course architect Gil Hanse succeeded in mimicking the natural swells and hollows of the native terrain, and only at the corners of the doglegs — I count eight or nine of them — do you detect artifice. The sand bunkers tucked into those corners are both deeper and larger than the natural grassy depressions they replace. But without steep inclines like Balcomie's to provide variety, a course laid out over these former crop fields required exaggeration of its natural features to avoid boredom. That's been nicely managed.

One of Craighead's deep bunkers — fun to see, not to visit.

Number one offers a good example. To reach the fairway your tee shot must carry 100 yards of waving, golden grasses the color of a palomino's mane, last year's ankle-deep stand gone to seed. From 170 to 235 yards off the tee a quartet of sandy bunkers defines the bend in the dogleg. A shot safely right of them finds an ample fairway. Too tight a line in trying to cut the corner and reach this 471-yard par five in two will find the bunkers. That's true on number four as well. Bunkers lie in wait where the fairway bends right 220 to 240 yards off the medal tees (but only 180 to 220 from the yellows). Simply turn and let fly, if you dare. With those bunkers awaiting any miscue, you'll need to measure risk against reward and think your way around this fairly open layout.

Add to the bunkers the depth of the uncut grasses in the deceptively difficult rough and the constant winds — no sheltering valleys here to offer respite — and you'll understand why accuracy is a must. The fairways are wide enough on a calm day, but wind seems to narrow them to paths winding through the rough. After you've missed a few fairways and left a ball or two in the ankle-grabbing grass beside them you'll be a believer. The first cut of rough is only two inches high and might as well be called "fairway." The *real* rough beyond it, knee deep and dense, is trouble. You're either in the fairway or devoutly wish you were.

Unless you play with a Crail member who can guide you, consult the course-planner booklet to aim your tee shot. Number two looks straightaway, for example, if you fix your gaze on the wrong flag as I did. It's actually a sharp dogleg right, not made any easier when your tee shot's headed toward the wrong green. And six of the first seven holes are bordered by out of bounds. May Island is visible at the mouth of the Firth beyond number seven green. Nearer at hand, only yards off the putting surface, a pillbox gun emplacement recalls a time when the nearly abandoned military base off to the right was more important than the game played here now. Part of the land the base occupies was once home to the Sauchope links, Balcomie's predecessor. The former military base now serves as a sparsely inhabited industrial park.

Number eight heads back toward the pro shop, a straight 470-yard par four. That's right: par four, and 487 yards long from the medal tees! It's named Stringbag Alley, a name easier to remember than to understand.

Across a stone wall, ten and eleven share the meadowlike area with the closing four holes of Balcomie Links. Then it's back across the wall again for twelve, a dogleg left and the only dogleg whose corner isn't bunkered. There's no need. A stand of head-high gorse bordering the fairway all the way to green-side discourages any attempt to shave yards off the hole.

A high stone wall crosses between the tee and green on fourteen, fifteen, and sixteen and serves as a backdrop to the heavily bunkered green at the par-three seventeenth, with its a two-tiered putting surface. Number eighteen heads back toward the tall flagpole beside the first tee.

Take time to stop in at the pro shop on your way to the car park and express your pleasure with the "new" course. Staff members are justifiably proud of Craighead and enjoy visitors' appreciation. Start by saying, "It's not Balcomie, but . . ." and they smile. They like what they know you're about to say.

Cupar Golf Club, founded in 1855, may be the oldest nine-hole club in Britain. The course on which members currently play, however, opened in 1892, after a falling out with the farmer from whom they leased the land on which Allan Robertson of St. Andrews laid out their original course. This "new" course, then, is more than a century old. Only 4,518 yards from the yellow tees (5,074 from the tips), it's a real test at par 62, owing to a number of deep bunkers, the sloping hillside fairways, and several canted greens.

You walk up a narrow paved road to the course, passing through a well-tended cemetery with row after row of engraved memorials at either hand. The course is inviting, and this approach to it a chance for thoughtful preparation. The pair of golfers I met on their way down this driveway leaving the course offered a tip: accuracy matters on these sidehill fairways, as does course management. Think your way around. No more than two holes at Cupar call for a driver. If you lack the willpower to keep your driver in the bag, leave it with the starter.

The course opens with a blind 140-yard tee shot to a green backed by a deep gully. An out of bounds on the right at the cemetery wall recalls a similar layout at Ballybunion in Ireland, where an opening tee shot sliced out of bounds that caroms off a headstone back into play is termed a "Lazarus." There are no easy resurrections at Cupar; the wall here is much higher. Trouble lies behind this green, as well. You won't know whether you've avoided both threats until you top the ridge and locate your ball.

Number two starts us upward for seven hillside holes until we make the descent back at nine. The second hole is 250 yards long, bunkered in the fairway and ending at a deep, flat, double green, shared with four. From here on we play back and forth across the face of the hill over lush fairways, with the market town of Cupar on display below.

The third, with its right-to-left sloping fairway, is flanked by out of bounds

Finishing the round at Cupar — Scotland's oldest 9-hole course.

both on the left (that cemetery again, this time daring you to hook) and beyond the green. It's a plateau green, a level putting surface jutting out of the hillside as once all of them did, before members decided that variety called for some greens (the fifth and eighth) to slope like the terrain.

By now you'll envy those West Virginia cattle you've heard about, born with long legs on one side, short on the other, so they can walk the sidehill trails without tipping over. Expect uneven lies. The ball will be lower or higher than your feet on every hole. If you find yourself in a level stance, you're either on a tee box, on a green, or have wandered off the course.

The longest hole on the course at 391 yards (368 for us), number five has the toughest canted green as well. The elevated tee box at number seven, a 340-yard par four, offers the best view of the town and the valley north and west. But the second shot is testing: a blind shot into a green described as "sloping" by those who somehow get their approach to hold the green, "treacherous" by those who don't.

The view from the number nine tee is enticing as well, down the broad fairway. It's an easy stroll. But at 225 yards it's a tough enough par three, even if it is downhill. From the medal tees it's a 257-yard par four, but not much easier for that extra stroke. Add to this another complication: the green slants not only left to right but also away from the approaching golfer. The best long iron or fairway wood tee shot will land short and thread its way among six lurking bunkers. The ball will drain to the back of the green, but that offers some faint consolation: the resulting putt is uphill.

Looking back up the slope from the cottagelike clubhouse, you'll be forgiven a little smugness if you've bested a hole or two at Cupar. An interesting nine-hole course, on the edge of a handsome town, nestled in a beautiful valley, Cupar is worth a visit.

11   Dora

The municipal course in the village of Cowdenbeath, six miles east of Dunfermline, occupies the site of a former coal mine. The mine had been named for the colliery manager's wife, Dora, and so is the course. Opened in 1988 at nine holes, the Dora course expanded to eighteen holes ten years later.

This 6,201-yard, par-72 course offers broad fairways and few bunkers . . . in general, an open and easy layout. Interest is created at several spots throughout the course by heavy curtains of foliage — evergreens as well as thick stands of birch — separating fairways from one another and creating a sense of privacy.

Holes one and two — straight, short, and level — were both part of the original nine and get us off to a slow start. The front side perks up at numbers four, a downhill par three, and five, a longish par four whose green is tucked off to the left and requires a long iron or fairway wood approach over a corner of rough. Small mounds create a background that frames the green. The next two par fours, six and seven, let us imagine what the newer nine will look like when the large planted areas have matured. At the moment those fairway-separating areas are islands of shrubbery and saplings.

The eighth is called The Pond. Roughly 230 yards off the tee on this 430-yard par four lies a pond in the right rough. Unseen from the tee, marshy rough reaches left from the pond into the fairway and creates the first problem on this long hole by invisibly narrowing the landing area. The second problem is a blind shot to a green lying beyond the crest of a hill, in this case tucked behind a bunker to the right of the apparent fairway. Hit it straight up the middle . . . and you've missed the green. You'll know the line the next time you play Dora, but the first time you play here the layout will cost a stroke. Or two. Number nine is Hit and Hope, a seemingly easy 143-yard par three; but the small green is two-tiered, the upper tier nestled behind a sand bunker and a large mound.

A fine shot — with no one here to see it.

The second nine preserves much of Dora's original layout. The fairway grass and rough here are thicker and the trees taller — all in all a better track to play. The only par five on the course is here at number seventeen, in the midst of seven fours. "Foulford," number eighteen, leads back to the clubhouse. It's probably just as well that the original reason for its name isn't obvious today.

For now, Dora feels generic; there's not much here to entice visitors, although there's nothing "wrong" with the course, either. A few years of growth may enrich it. We'll see.

12 Drumoig

Eight miles north of St. Andrews is a new facility named the Scottish National Golf Center, a title that might just as appropriately be applied to the complex of courses and extensive new practice facilities at St. Andrews, or even to the whole of Fife. The center opened in March of 1999 and includes a sales shop and driving range. In addition to taking lessons on the range and working on the putting green or nearby short game area, you can play badminton, table tennis, basketball, or volleyball, use the "fitness suite," or improve your sand game at two indoor bunkered greens, each activity for a fee. The 24-room hotel a quarter of a mile up the hill will attract visitors, especially given its friendly staff. A new manager had its original pink stucco exterior painted a less gaudy lemonade yellow. Good decision.

The real reason to visit Drumoig is the course. This par-72, eighteen-hole course is 7,006 yards long from the medal tees, a testing 6,376 from the tees we play. It opened in July 1996 and surrounds a protected wetland area visible from several holes but out-of-bounds in order to preserve the rare plants present there. The fairways are wide, the rough not much of a threat apart from the stands of easily avoided gorse that crown several fairway-side mounds. And the course promises to be even better for later generations. Thousands of trees have been planted to delineate areas separating the broad fairways. Most are chest-high now, in hundred-plant patches, inviting a return visit after they've had time to mature.

The fours are manageable, only two of them longer than 400 yards. The fives range from 499 to 530 yards in length. Only the par threes lack variety of distance. At 191, 183, 184, and 183 yards, they call for essentially the same club, wind allowing.

On the front side, the fifth and ninth are the standouts, marked as the numbers one and three stroke index. The printed course guide exaggerates by calling the 530-yard number five "one of the toughest par fives in the world.

A perfectly framed green — one of Drumoig's two "quarry" holes.

Third shot into a natural quarry. A very picturesque hole." Gorse is up to the left, and a climbing fairway ends in the natural amphitheater or "quarry" that names the hole. It's "toughest" not in design but because of the prevailing winds in your face. On a recent round in high winds I hit driver, driver, driver, and a punched nine-iron to reach the green. The parallel sixth hole, running back downslope and appropriately named "Downwind," required only driver, wedge to reach the green 409 yards away. The last hole on this side takes off from an elevated tee, heads between a pair of lakes, and takes a dogleg left turn into the green, calling for a second shot that skirts the edge of the lake; it's all laid out at your feet as you stand on the tee.

On the back nine notice number twelve, not for any special difficulty but for its name, "Pickletillum," after a village glimpsed in the distance. "West Quarry," the other side of the natural stone amphitheater that names number five, is an uphill dogleg left to a second quarry green. And the two closing holes take you into the prevailing wind for a par five and a par four. A pond or lake lies beyond each green. Have your card in shape before reaching seventeen and eighteen. Birdies will be rare on either hole.

This is a fine course, already scheduled to host Scottish championship play and likely to improve with age. It offers a respite from the crowds queuing up at the Old Course, and gives you the chance to play an upland layout your friends haven't seen, halfway between St. Andrews and Carnoustie.

13   the dukes

In 1990 the handsome Old Course Hotel reopened after a £16 million renovation. Located on the seventeenth at The Old Course, the "Road Hole," it
has become a magnet for individual visitors to St. Andrews as well as golf tour
groups. Even though it has expanded since 1999, when it had 125 rooms, it's
still full much of the time. Hotel management faced a problem. Play in the
Links Complex had become so heavy, especially over The Old Course, that
hotel guests could no longer be guaranteed tee times. The solution to that
problem was simple, though not easy. The Old Course Hotel acquired 330
acres two miles inland from the complex and built a new course, The Dukes,
with special rates and the first rights to tee times going to Old Course Hotel
guests.

Five-time Open champion Australian Peter Thomson designed a handsome, lengthy, but eminently fair championship course: 7,271 yards from the
medal tees, 6,749 for us, more than long enough. The Dukes Course is part
of St. Andrews only tangentially, by virtue of its connection with the Old
Course Hotel, but it offers a welcome option at this eastern tip of Fife. If the
courses of St. Andrews, Balcomie Links at Crail, and the new Kingsbarns give
you your fill of links golf, the nearest inland course is The Dukes, a good test
of your game.

The fairways are broad and generally undulating, with more obvious
mounds — not merely undulations — marking the border between fairways
and rough. The original printed course guide illustrates how the nines differ.
Because the holes that Thomson considered the back nine were ready for play
first, the course guide was printed showing holes ten through eighteen as the
opening nine. Visiting the course a year after it opened, Thomson asked management to return to his planned numbering scheme. A new version of the
course guide has been printed. I have one old edition, one new edition, and

Peter Thomson's design, a handsome par 3.

one even newer third edition, reflecting the fact that two holes have been lengthened.

We start on Highland, the opening hole in the architect's conception but number ten in the original guide. It's a comfortable par five at 479 yards with five bunkers, the first placed dead center in the fairway 240 yards off the tee. The last bunker protects the front of the green in the midst of a large mound. Thomson has expressed the belief that golfers ought to see hazards from far enough away to have the chance to avoid them, and suffer the consequences if they don't. With all the information laid out in front of you on this opening hole, you choose your weapons. Two woods, an iron to the center of the large green, two putts, and there you are: with a par to start, your confidence up and your swing loose and comfortable, you're ready to take on the course.

Burn Brig, opening the other nine, differs intriguingly; it's not so straightforward and is more demanding. A dogleg left par four at 429 from the tips ("only" 403 from the members' tee), it features whin-covered mounds and out of bounds on the left to threaten the tee shot, whin and out of bounds on the right for the second, as well as a burn to carry. It's a more complicated hole, requiring better management than Highland, which would be fine for mid-round after you've joined the flow of the course layout, but it's not an ideal opener. Thomson was right.

Four par fives, four threes, ten fours . . . in that way The Dukes is a standard eighteen. But each hole has its own character, each nine its standout hole (although we may disagree as to which one that is). Number seven, "Denbrae," is a par four at 431 yards, slightly downhill, with a group of four bunkers on the right tucked among six or seven mounds, just where the greedy will dump their tee shots if they try to shave the corner. Once past that trap, the golfer has an open shot to a raised circular green, rimmed at the back by four small mounds. Denbrae has a flowing feel about it as it curls around the bunkers and heads toward the cup.

On the back, the fourteenth hole demands a decision on the tee. Another long four at 435, "Well" is a potentially nondescript hole made distinctive by a well left-center of the fairway (with a burn running away from it to the right), and a single huge sycamore right-center, both of them 200 yards off the tree. The flag is visible in the distance, but only through the leafy corona of that tree, which effectively halves the fairway. There were originally three choices here; aim for the sycamore and hope to land short and roll past it on the right . . . but not as far as the burn; aim for the narrow gap between the sycamore and the well, hoping you hit the driver dead straight; or aim left of the well, leaving a second shot of more than 200 yards along the left rough, over mounds, into a depressed green only partly visible.

The first option has been foreclosed by two 30-tree islands of pines planted right of the sycamore. Now you must go left of the tree. After trying the two remaining options and failing at both, I've decided to lay up with a fairway wood off the tee next time and play Well as a five or, with luck and a good wedge shot, a one-putt four.

The fours here average 399 yards from the members' tees. When we see a tournament televised from The Dukes — and that's bound to come along soon — the competitors will play the fours at an average 428, with the longest at 448, more like a five for many of us.

One final characteristic leads to my only cavil about the course. Seven of the greens, six of them on the back nine, are two-tiered, a fact that counters Thomson's comment quoted in the course guide that "putting should be fun on generally flat surfaces." On six of the seven, tiering adds interest to the hole and may even derive from the original terrain.

But on the eighteenth, that's not the case. Thirty-seven yards deep, the final green rises what looks to be six feet from front to rear, nearly four feet of that in a single steep step. I doubt that Thomson wanted the pin placed at the top edge of that step, where it stood the first time I played The Dukes. Hit the putt hard enough to send it climbing the step and it rolls to the rear apron and probably off the green. Leave it an inch short of the step top and the ball curls around and speeds twenty feet past you headed back toward the tee. Twice fail to top the step and reach the upper level and you'll be inventing some interesting nicknames for the greenskeeper.

Golfers will enjoy this fine course . . . or at least the first 6,740 yards of it. Enjoying the final nine yards depends entirely on pin placement.

At the moment, it's easy enough to play The Dukes. As more visitors come to know it, that may be less true, although guests at The Old Course Hotel — who have first call on tee times here — will still focus their attention on the links complex outside their windows. For them, as for us, The Dukes is a backup course, but a fine one.

14   Dunfermline

The Dunfermline Club was formed in 1887, but the course in play at Pitferrane, Crossford (a mile west of Dunfermline, proper), is the fourth venue for club members. It succeeded a course designed by James Braid on the Torrie estate (more of which later); and over the years the club has been home to a number of well-known golfers. Two Dunfermline members, Robert Reid and Robert Lockhart, were instrumental in forming the first U.S. golf club, the St. Andrews, in Yonkers, New York. Another member, Miss Joan Lawrence, former Curtis Cup team member and thrice consecutively the Scottish Ladies Champion, has been Captain at Aberdour. Not *Lady* Captain. Club Captain.

The unique clubhouse at Dunfermline draws attention at once. A towering dun-colored stone building of five stories, it's more than 600 years old and has been in the Halkett family since the fourteenth century. A single-story modern extension is integrated nicely into the base of the towering structure to house the bar, lounge, and locker room. The pro shop, until recently tucked into the original Halkett family chapel, now stands alone in a matching one-story building some forty yards away.

Today's dining room, located at the top of a circular stone stair, beyond a dark foyer rich with ornately carved oak walls, deserves a visit, if only to see the portraits of the Halkett family carved into the dining room shutters. Other rooms of the original building have been modernized and now house the Dunfermline Club chef and his family. They share their quarters, staff members will explain, with the ghost of a Halkett lady who threw herself off the tower in a fit of despair over an illicit love affair.

The course itself is a charmer, a highly regarded inland eighteen. Near-championship quality, it offers a range of interesting holes, with age creating a distinctive characteristic (like the following), as well as the charm. More recent courses, seeded and sodded with grasses developed specifically for golf courses, achieve a unified color and lush texture, even in the rough. In older

A six-hundred-year-old clubhouse, on the right, the two-year-old pro shop on the left — a perfect sand shot in mid-air.

courses like Dunfermline's, however, the roughs are comprised of a range of grasses selected by wind, weather, and innate hardiness. Such differing grasses give a mottled appearance to the rough that may belie its generally even texture, but they confer the benefit of clearly distinguishing rough from fairway. This course displays the work of a fine grounds crew. It seems in better shape at each new visit and is a comfortable course, the holes nicely varied and pleasant to walk.

The opening nine is higher, with fairways threading through mature plantings of chestnut and birch and rhododendron (a landscaping plant in Pennsylvania, a "weed" in Scotland). Two of the first three holes offer the chance for birdie: the 275-yard opening par four, and number three, a par five but only 465 yards long. They sandwich between them a 190-yard downhill par three. This opening trio is the place to build a cushion on the card as a hedge against trouble lying in wait ahead.

With five fives and five threes scattered through the round you won't easily settle into a groove. The front nine holds no consecutive par fours, and then the back — lower in elevation than the front and nearly meadowland — begins with three in a row. Each hole sets a new challenge, especially the par threes. Number five, The Cadger's Stane, may be the toughest par on the course, though the scorecard calls it stroke number fifteen. At only 160 yards, it's uphill and can play two clubs longer than the card reads. The putting surface is hidden, bunkered close on the left, and it falls off sharply to the right. Be content if you give back no more than one of the strokes you saved on the first three holes.

On the back nine, number thirteen is another tough par three, uphill to a mounded green, with four a respectable score. A definition posted in the St. Andrews British Golf Museum reminds us that "bogey" doesn't mean "failure to make par." It means the score a good amateur achieves. For any but a scratch golfer, the word "bogey" is more boast than apology.

The ideal round at Dunfermline might record eighteen fours on the card, with bogeys on the threes and birdies on the fives, however tough that would be to manage on the closing two par fives. Number seventeen is a sharp dogleg right with two blind shots, one uphill off the tee, one steeply downhill to a hidden flag. Cross the ridge too far left with your tee shot and you drive through the fairway into heavy rough. No getting home from there. The second shot demands precision as well. A target circle high atop an aiming pole marks the unseen green far below the fairway. Here underclubbing is the problem, because the foreshortening effect of the raised target can confuse club selection.

On eighteen the issue is simply length — 529 yards from the tips and 480 from the medal tees — over a soft fairway. What the drive carries is all you can depend on; don't expect help from the roll. Few golfers will putt for eagle here, although a one-putt birdie is still possible.

But then, we didn't come to Dunfermline expecting an even-par round. It's pleasure enough to gauge and enjoy the course. Take the published pro guide with you and heed the tips printed there. The variety and imagination in J. R. Stutt's design (he did Glenrothes as well) make Dunfermline a good choice among Fife's inland courses.

Consider a full-day outing. Golf early, lunch in a 600-year-old oak-walled dining room, and play a second round over the same track, applying the morning's lessons.

15 ðunnikier park

Like Auchterderran, the Dunnikier Park golf course is one of the six municipal courses managed by the Kirkcaldy Council. It contends with Glenrothes for the unofficial title of best of the lot. At 6,709 yards, par 71, this eighteen-hole course is one that many private clubs would be pleased to play. Some do.

A relatively young club, Dunnikier and its 500-plus members are housed in their own clubhouse adjacent to a private hotel on the park grounds, once part of the Oswald Estate. Like the hotel at Balbirnie Park, this hotel was the manor house on a large private estate but has been acquired for public use. Across the car park shared by club members and visitors are the starter's shack and its ball rack, a familiar device that's disappearing from U.S. public courses. Walk up, drop your ball into the top end of the pipe, and wait for it to roll into view at the bottom end. It's your turn at the first tee.

Dunnikier's fairways are broad and the greens in fine condition despite heavy play. Credit Fife's frequent rains for the lush grass and the thick stands of fir, spruce, and chestnut trees bordering the fairways.

Every course has a distinctive trait about it, and at Dunnikier it's the bunkers. Although they're not especially difficult, both their design and placement are unique. Shaped like large clams with the top shell opened at the hinge to stand upright, they front or flank every green, creating hurdles to overcome. The green is mounded beyond the bunker's raised back lip. From the tee box the back rim of a green-fronting bunker looks as high as the flag. It's actually "only" chest high, though still not inviting when you find yourself standing in the sand. Number eleven, a 150-yard par three, offers examples of the impact bunker location can have. A bunker right front, another on the left, means a narrow opening between them for golfers who run their shots in. Fly one to the green and you risk a severe kick off the bunker-back slope. The undulations they create complicate putting as well.

All the driving holes at Dunnikier except nine and eighteen have bunkers

Fife's Double-Loop Courses

BALBIRNIE PARK
CHARLETON
DRUMOIG
THE DUKES
DUNNIKIER PARK
KINGSBARNS
LADYBANK
SCOTSCRAIG
ST. MICHAEL'S

The clam-shaped bunkers of Dunnikier Park.

narrowing the landing area for your tee shot. Someone long enough may carry them. Those more cautious will steer clear or even lay up short. Either way, the challenge is obvious. A pair of bunkers at the fairway edges 190 yards off the tee can narrow a broad fairway to less than thirty yards. It's like driving through the pinched waist of an hourglass.

The course opens with a drive uphill toward a striped post, an omen of things to come. Blind tee shots start off numbers seven and eight, a pair of parallel par fours at 351 yards each, as well as several other holes. After each blind shot, hit the next — or putt out and walk off the green — then ring the iron-pipe gong hanging nearby. Invite the following group to hit up. In the midst of Dunnikier's anvil chorus, it takes attentiveness to identify the clanging meant for you.

Number seventeen, for example, is 363 yards long with a blind second shot into a small bunkered green only 70 yards or so beyond a ridge. Waiting to hit that blind approach, listen for the gong, wait a moment for the group ahead to clear, then aim for the sound and fire away.

There are two par fives on the front nine, only one on the back, but the 467-yard par-four eighteenth plays like another. Downhill, up, and down again, it's a testing finish to the round. This is a public course but not a pushover.

If you find yourself in Kirkcaldy, ask for directions to Dunnikier Park. It's a well-conditioned course that's easy to enjoy, along with the Scots you'll meet there.

16 eLie

In a recently published brochure the Fife tourist board tells us that the Elie course has been played since 1589. Club members temper that unprovable boast. It's true that the Burgh of Earlsferry was issued a charter in 1589 specifically granting the "right of golf." But the earliest date it has been proven that golf was played over this stretch of links land is 1750, an impressive enough date, a generation before our Declaration of Independence.

The course we play today was actually completed in 1895. James Braid, five-time Open champion, played over these links as a boy, joined the Earlsferry Thistle Club here when he was fifteen in 1885, was involved in planning the course layout (designed by Auld Tom Morris), and had a hand in its revision 30 years later, making it one of the 300 courses to benefit from his sense of design. He was elected a life member here in 1937. All that is the equivalent of saying someone named James Braid played at Elie, just as someone named Bobby Jones was associated with American golf.

It's not only its heritage that makes Elie remarkable. The pleasure starts on the first tee, if you enjoy a gallery. Club members at the clubhouse windows watch you tee off. Once you've hit over the brow of the steep, knobby hillside thrown up before you like a blanket billowing on a clothesline, you climb out of sight of the clubhouse, but not out of the starter's view. That 30-year veteran mans a 1938 submarine periscope installed high above the starter's shack after World War II. It allows him to see when the way's clear to send the next golfer off the tee. Once past the ridge, if you find your ball caught in one of the pockets or swales or depressions more suited to a goat's footing than yours, be aware that you'll play the shot in front of a gallery of one and be grateful for his practiced tact. No one will know from him how awkward you look to begin this round.

The first two holes — headed inland, then back out — have fairways with turf warped and twisted beyond anticipation. All the gouges and gullies are

Wind off Ruby Bay stirs the knee-high rough.

the result of former coal mining digs on one and two. They reach into fairway eighteen as well, just as peat harvesting from some courses in Ireland has left trenches and burns that go nowhere. The second hole at Elie comes back over that ridge again to the green and reveals the sea just beyond the rank of rooftops that parallels number three fairway. The sea is with us from this point on through most of the round.

One old hand here calls Elie serene in the sunshine, a monster in the wind and rain. To know the course you have to play it at both extremes, and — with luck or good planning — a range of weather conditions in between. Learning the course really begins at the 213-yard par-three third. Turn right off number two green and the sea now lies at your left past the palisade of houses. It also waits dead ahead, beyond the deception of what seems a level stretch of land. From here on the wind murmurs or howls but is rarely still. And that level-seeming land is never really level. Each shot is an adventure, as your ball bounds in devious and unexpected caroms, darting left or right off fairway undulations.

The course is 6,273 yards long, par 70, with no par five and only two threes. That's right: two threes, and sixteen par fours! Without constant reference to the scorecard, it's hard to believe. Each hole is different, and each plays as the day's conditions allow. That same old-timer says of the par-four number twelve, for example, "A par five today, maybe a six." Any stretch of 466 yards is challenge enough, crosswind. Into the wind, even a six is an ambitious goal. Number three is one of the two par threes; the other is eleven. All the fours range in distance from three shorter than 300 yards to six longer than 400.

I count 80 sand-filled bunkers and estimate scores of grassy bowls and depressions; but the fairways are broad enough, only slightly dog-legged if at all, and the greens more than fair. They tend to be level, except for those shaped like a saucer to collect an approach shot.

There is striking pleasure everywhere. Number seven, for instance, is "Peggy's," a downwind par four of 252 yards. Avoid the bunker at the left front of the green — draw your tee shot into the pin rather than fading it — and you'll have the satisfaction of a two-putt birdie or even an eagle on this par four . . . on a sometime Open-qualifying course!

The second nine has a similar opportunity. "Lundar Law," number ten, is listed on the card at 288 yards. But a drive crossing the crest of the ridge 225 yards ahead will pitch forward down a steeply two-tiered hill face and fetch up near or even on the green. Crossing the ridge leads to a wonderful view of the rocky escarpment left of the green and skellies in Ruby Bay, where grunting, barking seals sun themselves. The course turns to parallel the coast at number eleven. The tee is near the seals' playground, with the green dead ahead and frigid waves on the left.

The longest par four on the course is number twelve, reachable by most only on calm days. And thirteen has a shallow, elevated green that probably won't hold a long approach. A shot hit intentionally over the green (by those who have the nerve to hit the extra club or two) can curl back down off the side of number fourteen tee onto the putting surface.

The next three holes are usually down or across the wind, and the hardest work of the course is now behind us. "Ferry," the seventeenth, calls for two long shots that avoid out of bounds on the left.

The eighteenth hole — named "Home" — presents a mounded, uneven fairway, with five well-placed bunkers and deep-grass rough on the low right side of the fairway waiting to remind you who's in charge here. Because the windows of the clubhouse overlook the eighteenth green as well as the first tee, expect to have a gallery. Par the hole, and those watching will understand the spring in your step. Birdie it, and you'll know how James Braid or course record holder Kel Nagle felt. Often.

For those who've played many of the courses in the Kingdom, Elie ranks very near the top of the list.

eLie sports cLuB

Family golf at Elie.

As early as 1770 there was a short course as well as a long course at Elie. Although the short course was not the layout today called the Elie Sports Club, it's reassuring to know that attention was paid that long ago to what some consider a "beginner's course," but one that is both more challenging and more interesting than the St. Andrews' Balgove nine. The Sports Club complex includes a putting green, a driving range, a half-dozen tennis courts, and a nine-hole course.

On a recent stop at Elie I watched three family groups tee off on the Sports Club's first hole. It parallels Elie's number one seaward across the fence. At 341 yards it's only a sand wedge shorter than Elie's "Stacks" next door and plays over a broader, more hospitable fairway.

It's that way around the nine, with no hole longer than the number one "Plantation." With five threes and four fours, the layout might be called an "executive" course in the States, but that doesn't necessarily mean it's easy. The par threes require tee shots of 195, 187, 179, 217, and 166 yards, all in the same winds that blow over the long course next door, and the fours stretch to 341, 261, 335, and 296.

Playing when Elie is crowded (the club now employs a lottery system for tee times in mid-summer), playing with less experienced partners, or playing when short of time — when 100 minutes of golf is possible but 200 is not — you'll enjoy this course. PGA pro Robin Wilson and his staff will make you welcome, as they do the Elie and Earlsferry Club members who share access to this pro shop and benefit even more than do casual visitors to the Elie Sports Club.

17 Elmwood

In Fife golf courses are so plentiful that in 1997 a reader of the St. Andrews weekly newspaper the *Citizen* wrote to complain of the problem in reaching seaside paths without dashing through a golf course dodging missiles. The Firth-view coast of the county is being controlled by a single special-interest group, the letter writer lamented. Links courses are barriers to reaching the beach, not links, and even in golf-rich Fife more courses are about to open, or are under construction, or are being contemplated.

When she wrote, there was no Elmwood Golf Course, where play began in May of 1998. I learned about the course in the Fife *Herald* only months later, when it was the newest course in Fife . . . though it wasn't for long. Kingsbarns wears that title now, with others about to open, under construction, or being contemplated.

The second pay-as-you-play course in the Kingdom, after Charleton, Elmwood was also designed by Charleton's designer, former R&A captain John Salvesen. At Charleton he had had more to work with: established forests, a running burn, stone walls, and marked changes in elevation. Elmwood, on the other hand, lies on gently rolling former farm fields belonging to Elmwood College a mile or two west of Cupar. It lacks water and has few bunkers, little change in elevation, and few mature trees (though 20,000, from seedlings to saplings, have been planted on the course). At 5,653 yards in length from the yellow tees, par 70, it's not very long. Five of the seven par fours on the back nine are less than 300 yards. How can such a course be made interesting?

First, it's a laboratory for more than 400 students in the greenskeeping program at Elmwood College. Picture a course with 400 pairs of hands to keep it in shape. It ought to be in top condition, and it is. Second, it's seldom (probably never) crowded or worn by excessive play. Last year it hosted 20,000 rounds and it anticipates 25,000 next year. Busy, but not crowded.

Both a golf course and a laboratory — for four hundred apprentice greenskeepers.

More important, the course achieves interest in a way rarely so consistently pursued: the fairways are not mowed as the crow flies, even when holes are laid out in straight lines. It's not obvious whether this trait is owed designer Salvesen or course manager and greenskeeper John Quinn, but I'd say that Quinn's contribution has been significant.

Number three, for instance, a 170-yard par three, is mowed as if it were a slight right-to-left dogleg. A golfer seduced by the fairway's appearance will leave his tee shot short or to the right. Flying a shot to the pin takes it over a swath of first-cut rough intruding from the left and over a sand bunker tucked into the left front of the green. Probably not a problem.

But number four is a 440-yard hole mowed in an unobtrusive S-curve. With rough reaching into the fairway first from one side and then from the other, the fairway is actually narrowed to half its apparent width. That's an unsolvable problem, if it's unrecognized. Hit it straight down the narrowed center, if you can; but the hole actually plays more like target golf than not.

Fairway definition throughout the course is very clear. The grass is cut close. First-cut rough is two inches deep. The six- to eight-inch second cut hides your shoes and could worry U.S. Open survivors. Ignoring the way each hole is mowed can mean playing into and out of punishing rough. On Elmwood's fairways a straight line may be the shortest distance between two points; it's also the riskiest. And each hole requires a tee shot carrying 75 yards over grassy rough simply to reach the fairway.

Without departing from this pattern, number eleven adds another wrinkle. The longest hole on the course at 526 yards from the tips, it leads (down the S-cut fairway) to a sloping green beyond a deep, foreshortening depression, site of a newly introduced burn that was not here when I first played Elmwood. Take an extra club and hit to the pin, or past. Anything short curls back off the green into that grassy bowl toward the burn.

A similar interesting hole on the back is the 253-yard par-four sixteenth, blind tee shot and all. Catch your drive on the sweet spot, send it past the black-and-white aiming pole, and trudge over the brow of the hill hoping to putt. Unless your tee shot is dead center, it's hung up in a patch of first-cut rough narrowing the fairway from the left. If it's dead center, the ball may well stop in a depression short of the green. The sixteenth hole is a model of subtlety. It looks like a pushover but doesn't play like one.

The course, overall, doesn't either. Instead it demonstrates how the partnership of architect and greenskeeper can impact your game. Whether it was Salvesen or Quinn (and it was probably both), someone has turned a potentially nondescript course into one you'll want to play again, if only to understand and overcome its subtle deceptions. And the fine condition of the Elmwood course has attracted enough attention that Quinn's crew has been retained to maintain the next course we visit, Falkland.

18 FALKLAND

The village of Falkland — since 1458 a royal burgh — sits against the base of the East Lomond Hills in a valley marked by neat walled fields and pastures. Tourists visit the sixteenth-century Falkland Palace located on the site of the twelfth-century Macduff's Castle. Only two or three streets away the nine-hole Falkland course surrounds a football pitch on land once a rubbish dump but reclaimed by club members' efforts. The pride they take in that common effort is echoed in the care the course is given, for the past few years that care provided by a crew from Elmwood College under a special contract.

Par is 68, at 5,020 yards for two trips around this nine-hole layout. Five of the first six holes are flat, straight, narrow, and short. Only number two, a 476-yard par five, has length enough to ameliorate its blandness . . . usually. On football days, we actually tee off beyond the mid-course football (read "soccer") field, and the hole is thus shortened by some 120 yards.

By the time you reach number seven, the only dogleg on the course, you're so accustomed to peering straight down the fairway looking for the flag that you may not spot the seventh green off to the left. But the dogleg here is unexpected rather than rewarding, arbitrary rather than appropriate, since it follows no feature in the terrain.

The eighth offers a moment's interest. A par three of 148 yards, it ends at a two-tiered green and is backed by a long view of the East Lomond Hills in the distance. Similarly, number nine, "Palace," is named for and made more interesting by the target beyond it. You may have to delay your tee shot on nine until number one fairway clears, because the opening and closing holes share the same fairway for much of their length. They also share a burn-crossing arched stone bridge, more interesting inbound than out because of the view. Behind the ninth green stands Falkland Palace, the reason most visitors come to this small village.

Falkland Palace, an aiming spire behind 9 green.

We may admire the handsome central village square itself, the lush green surrounding countryside, and the fine condition of this small nine. But, given the splendid options for play available elsewhere in Fife, those attractions won't elevate this flat meadowland course very high on your list of preferred courses.

19   GLENROTHES

Officially opened in 1968, a year after construction had been completed, the council-managed public Glenrothes course occupies 160 acres and plays to a par 71 over its 6,444-yard length. Designer J. R. Stutt enriched the site with 52,000 trees and 9,000 shrubs, many clumped by species in groves, when he turned this patch of pasture west of the city into a hilly upland course.

The city of Glenrothes resembles the "new towns" built three generations ago within commuting range of London. At each roundabout on the main road through town signs point the way toward industrial complexes and high-tech business parks. Next to a Safeway on the east edge of town stands an outlet of most Americans' favorite "Scottish" restaurant—McDonalds, the first I've seen in Fife. One of the roundabouts near the course is named "Detroit." Passing between ranks of handsome flats and new schools you find the streets broad, directional signs plentiful, traffic brisk, and shoppers striding rather than strolling. Glenrothes looks and feels like a "new town."

The Glenrothes course manages to blend the "new" character of the city with the golfing traditions of rural Fife. It offers ample on-site parking that disappears behind us as we pass beyond the first green into the forested hills beyond. And raised and squared-off tee boxes point the way along fairways shaped by natural forces rather than by a squadron of bulldozers.

One Scottish practice less common in the States—a British tradition, in fact—involves the naming of holes. At Glenrothes you tee off toward "Benarty View" and pass on to the second hole on "Goatmilk Hill." "Wester Gales" lies just ahead, followed by "Pitcairn," the most picturesque fairway of them all. The left rough is a sweeping hillside of gorse, a brilliant glowing yellow for one quarter of the year, holly green to mahogany in color the other months. Number six, a 388-yard par four, promises to give us "Bluidyfits."

On the back nine a burn crosses four holes, one of them (number thirteen) in fact called "Carryburn." The toughest hole on the course may be the 447-

yard par four twelfth, confessionally named "Stutt's Curse" by designer J. R. Stutt. We head downhill, cross the burn (a 225-yard carry off the tee), and then climb 220 yards up the daunting hill to a plateau green whose surface isn't visible even on your probable third shot, a wedge or short iron aimed toward the visible flag and the top half of the flagstick. Anyone scrambling for a five or six might curse designer Stutts . . . though that's probably not what he meant when he named the hole.

I recently played the course with Jim, a retired Vietnam veteran and factory worker who knows all six of the council-managed courses in Fife. He enjoyed guiding a Yank around his favorite of the six and solved one of my problems. Like most Scottish courses, Glenrothes lacks distance markers. With a course planner I could have calculated yardages, but like other public courses, Glenrothes doesn't offer those handy booklets for sale. Jim didn't need one. Without specifying yards to the pin, he knew which club to hit. When I asked for his help, he looked up at the treetops and sniffed, as if he could see and smell the breeze, shrugged, and said "I'd be hitting a four-iron from here. You'll want a six."

His ability to judge distances is a skill I lack and need to develop. How many yards from here to carry the burn? It's no use depending on the tee box markers; many are faded or illegible. Some offer the distance in meters (110 percent of yardage). Unless you want the "Jim" you play with grinning behind the back of his hand, don't bring your $500 laser distance reader. Do what he does. Compare your iron shots to his, estimate the difference in length, and then watch what club he hits in order to select yours.

After that fails twice, ask his help.

With fairways broad and greens slow—some on the back nine are slow to the point of being shaggy—this is a course to attack. Forget finesse and play Jim's game. Go after Glenrothes and it rewards your boldness. Carry the burn. Shoot for the back of the green. Jim will respect your aggressiveness. It's the way he plays. I'll be ready when I meet him in Leven to play the Scoonie course with him.

There are no "gimmes" in Fife. Putt them all.

20 KINGHORN

Seve Ballesteros recently wished aloud that tournament fairways were narrowed to half their non-tournament width. That way, he said, all competitors would play their second shots out of the rough, as he does. Behind Seve's joke is an attitude that Auld Tom Morris, four-time British Open Champion and greenskeeper at St. Andrews for forty years, would have understood. The best golfers conquer the worst conditions. When asked in 1887 to evaluate the plot of links land chosen for the planned Kinghorn course, Auld Tom praised it for having a "sufficient number of natural hazards and undulations to relieve it from tameness and to test the skill of players." More than sufficient. The hilly, tumbled links of Kinghorn can reveal a golfer's talents, or expose his weakness.

This eighteen-hole municipal course shares with the nearby private courses at Burntisland and Aberdour views of the Firth, Edinburgh, and the Lomonds. It also shares chill winds off the Firth, frequent fogs (locally called "haar"), and the feeling of age and tradition. Play two or three holes of the course, let's say two with names like "Whang" and "Blue Scoot," and it wouldn't surprise you to meet a man in a tweed coat with a clutch of hickory-shafted clubs under one arm.

Auld Tom laid out the course. A greenskeeper was hired and handed a scythe and a hole-cutting iron, and play began. (How do you get a Stimp meter reading on a green mowed with a scythe?)

Over the years the course has changed many times, most interestingly in 1929, when it was extended to include three par sixes in its then total par of 79. The boundaries flexed and the length and number of holes increased and diminished until in 1965 Kinghorn finally became the course played today: eighteen holes over hills and through valleys, with only a single tree in sight . . . out of play off sixteen, behind the seventeenth tee.

Half the holes are straightaway; the other half include one or two blind

Pettycur Bay at hand, Edinburgh across the Firth.

shots each. They cross one another and defy the first-time golfer to understand where he is . . . or where he should be. After a steep climb to the green
of par-three number two, we turn back down the hill toward another par
three, but this one is tucked just behind a four-foot high stone wall that once
bordered farm fields and now bisects the course. Like the road (and wall) at
number seventeen on The Old Course, this wall is in play. No free drop here:
if your five- or six-iron on this 170-yard downhill hole doesn't clear the wall,
you have a flop shot to try. It had better be good: the green lies only six paces
past the wall, and a bladed wedge can carom back off that stone wall faster
than you can duck.

Number five is only 313 yards long but uphill and crossed by three ridges
that prevent any roll for the tee shot. Popular wisdom says that a stretch of
sandy beach grass–bearing soil is termed "links land" because it "links"

seashore to arable farmland. A placard in the British Golf Museum in St. Andrews (a must-visit for any golfer coming to Fife) says otherwise. "Links" comes from the word "hlincas," plural of the Old English word "hlinc," for "ridge." Whichever derivation of "links" is right, popular wisdom or scholarship, the fifth at Kinghorn qualifies. Its tumbled and twisted sandy ridges stretch from the Firth below to oat fields above.

If you have a camera in your bag, the third, twelfth, and seventeenth tees give the best view out over the Firth. Focusing on enjoying the vistas may keep your mind off what's happening to the scorecard. With ten fours and eight threes on the card (par 64), the total may not be a huge number. It's not likely to be a 64, either, not when the course record is 62.

A pair of threes ends the round, just as a pair of threes starts the round five miles down the coast at Aberdour. Here at Kinghorn the greens of seventeen and eighteen are hung on the hillside out over the coastal road, hidden from view below. They overlook Pettycur Bay, where sailboats lie canted on the mud at low tide and strain at their tethers when the tide is in. There is always wind on these two holes — inbound, outbound, across your line, or in your face — no matter what may be happening farther inland. The choice of club here depends on that wind, and on your imagination.

That's the trait needed here, not to defeat Kinghorn, but simply to earn a draw with this quirky course. Ballesteros has it, as do Phil Mickelson and others. It's a safe bet that Auld Tom Morris had it, and the Kinghorn course he designed demands it. Imagination.

The links course at Kingsbarns, six miles from St. Andrews and three from Crail, opened in July 2000 . . . for the second time. Play actually began over this seaside links land in 1793 and continued for 146 years until World War II, when R.A.F. use of the land closed the course in 1939. (One rumor claims that the Kingsbarns Club never disbanded and that its two or three surviving members — venerable worthies today — may yet play again over this wonderful piece of links land.) Former R&A secretary Sir Michael Bonallack calls this track "one of the last true seaside links sites capable of development in Scotland. It is an extraordinary setting."

I've not only played the course, but some months earlier I enjoyed a walking tour with developer and managing director Mark Parsinen, who collaborated with designer Kyle Phillips in planning and laying out the resurrected Kingsbarns. Parsinen's description of their intentions, along with his pride in the obvious day-by-day growth of the course, taught me more than several rounds of play on my own might have.

The first hole illustrates the design intentions here. The tee box is beside the clubhouse and the large practice putting green. From the tee, the sea is visible, as it is from every hole on the course. It's a constant part of the round, even when it's not in play. On this first hole, for instance, the slightly crowned green 425 yards from the tee seems backed hard against the sea. In fact it's 150 yards short of the water, but to the golfer's eye a wave-lapped out of bounds lurks just beyond the putting surface. Time after time the North Sea fills the frame beyond the golfer's target and tests his concentration.

From the first tee the green is visible above a large patch of heather just ahead on the right. The heather shouldn't come into play. On four holes, heather has been planted and is spreading as a visual feature, just as gorse and broom have been used effectively to define the slopes or crowns of dunes separating fairways. The rough has been carefully planned as well. It has been

The North Sea — visible from every hole at Kingsbarns.

planted with a mixture of meadow grass, sheep's fescue, and other grasses introduced atop nutritionally limited soils so that the rough won't thicken. Wild poppies have seeded themselves. The rough has already grown tall enough to seize an errant shot, yet it is not so thick that balls disappear into a snarl of weeds.

This opening par four can be played at a variety of lengths: 425 yards from the back, any length from 405 yards down to 370 off the medal tees, and as short as 305 yards from the forward tees. A 75-yard carry over wind-fluttered golden rough gets us to the ample green fairway. More than ample, it widens to 100 yards or more beyond a ridge of rough extending partway down the right side. Everyone on the short grass will have a second shot here, but to have a chance for a birdie there's really only one ideal spot on the fairway, left of left-center. Even from that spot the illusion of the sea lapping at the back of the green is likely to seduce some golfers into underclubbing rather than hitting into a danger that's only apparent.

So it goes around the course. The sea is always present, as are the sea breezes. At low tide the skellies poke their jumbled rocky ledges up from the water awash with breaking waves. Every hole has been planned with a "position A," but there are also broad landing areas from which par is possible but a birdie isn't likely.

Number two is a par three foreshortened in our view by a depression short of the green and, once again, the sea behind it. The third is a shortish par five (500 yards from the medal tees) along the seashore in a twisting swale between the dunes, like two or three of the coastal holes at Turnberry or Troon. Coming off number three green we double back inland, but at a raised level. The sea seems immediately next to us on the left; it's actually one fairway width away.

The course is laid out as a double loop, with a stop at the clubhouse possible between nines. From the clubhouse we see a stone bridge to eighteen green. It crosses a burn that's an interesting story in itself. The design of Kingsbarns called for the introduction of a mid-course burn to drain runoff into the sea. With excavations underway to create that feature, the architect discovered that the burn already existed, crossed by an arching stone bridge, buried eight feet underground. Prisoners taken in the Napoleonic Wars, research revealed, were used here as work crews. They filled in the natural depression in order to create more level land for farming and, in so doing, buried the burn. When it was discovered, with its hand-stacked stone sides and the bridge crossing it, Parsinen and Phillips incorporated their amazing find. Imagine how they felt to find their plans anticipated by the first creator of this links land. That's being *right!*

The back nine includes an area played in the original eighteenth-century layout here. Most interesting on this side are four holes laid out beyond a burn and a copse of seventy-foot-tall sycamores and massed rhododendron covering the forest floor. Numbers twelve and thirteen point toward Crail. Balcomie Links and the Crail clubhouse are visible in the distance along the shoreline, and this loop of two out, two back ends with the dramatic fifteenth.

A splendid finish to a memorable round.

It's a par three as long as 205 yards (or as short as 110) over the skellies at low tide, or blue water when the tide is in. The green is huge, five times as large as the typical stateside green. In fact, the greens throughout the Kingsbarns course average 1,100 square meters in area.

There's much to be said about what is probably the last new links course we will see in the Kingdom. Other inland courses are planned, but to play the seaside golf that brings most of us to Fife has already come to mean including this new and splendid layout. For generations golfers have driven past the Erskine estate and the Cambo farm here beside the North Sea on their way to Crail or back to St. Andrews, without knowing what lay only a half-mile off the road. Once they've driven down the access road and played this course it will no longer be a stopover on the way to somewhere else.

For many, the splendid links at Kingsbarns — "new," but 200 years old — will become their destination.

22   kirkcaLòy

Auld Tom Morris died in 1908 at the age of 86, outliving his son, Young Tom, by 33 years. A handful of names — Auchterlonie, Braid, Park, Robertson, and a few others — recur over and over in the history of Scottish golf, but none is heard more often than Tom Morris, champion golfer, ball maker, greenskeeper, and course designer. Turn a corner in Fife and you'll bump into his influence. He designed the Kirkcaldy course in 1904, at the age of 82.

The course has been tweaked since, but it still carries about it the mark of a traditional Scottish course. It seems not so much "created" as "discovered" here, especially the front nine, played since 1904 (the second nine was added two years later). The history of course modifications over the years is well documented. The only change we might sense today has to do with the original holes seven through ten (the Meadows), so often flooded that they were replaced by four holes on higher ground (the Fields), another part of the Raith Estate, whose lands these were.

Number one is a 90-degree dogleg left and up a hill, with the added challenge of a burn crossing the fairway just short of the landing area for your drive. Only 5,839 yards long, the course plays longer. Six of the holes call for a steep climb, making the available rental buggies an option to consider. Carry your clubs, pull a trolley, ride a buggy, or make the compromise of renting an electric-powered trolley. Halfway up the first fairway climb I was glad I'd compromised.

The second hole is a 230-yard par three with a blind tee shot. It's straight ahead. Your drive had better be. After a pair of fours at three and four made tough by the terrain, we drop down a service road to play five through nine in the Meadows. The fairways are narrow, the greens small, and the course continues to play longer than the card promises.

It's the turn from number six green, through a notch cut in a high stone ridge, that takes us into the heart of the original design. Short holes —

Imagine the climb to get here and look back at the new clubhouse.

120, 300, and 310 yards short — seven, eight, and nine are renumbered holes made difficult by being so narrow. On the right, a fast-running burn flanks all three holes. On the left of seven and eight a high rocky ridge covered with gorse and twisted hawthorns is the other jaw of the pinchers. Fly your tee shot onto the narrow seventh green, because there's next to no fairway for a shot falling short. At fifteen paces rock to river, it's more path than fairway.

Number eight is equally narrow for its first 100 yards or so, opening into a landing area perhaps twice that wide, if you can call 30 yards "wide." It's like trying to hit your tee shot into the end of a pipe. The hole is only 300 yards long. Consider a pair of mid-irons if you want to play number eight on the short grass, since even a conservative long iron pushed or pulled off dead center will cost strokes. Thinking "driver" here is smug folly.

It's a relief to play nine, with danger only on the right from the burn that Auld Tom incorporated into his design a century ago. Then we climb the service road again to take on number ten, called "Table." The narrow, flat green hung on the sloping hillside at the left is only 263 yards off the tee, downslope, and often downwind. It may be the best birdie chance on the course, time to let out the shaft.

From the eleventh tee we can see the Firth and the silhouette of Edinburgh beyond it. The holes here atop the area called the Fields also show us the 300-year-old great house of the Raith Estate on the highest hilltop off to the northeast. With Kirkcaldy below us masked from view by the mature forest of this parkland course, we're part of a scene little changed since the eighteenth century.

Both twelve and seventeen are par fives, 530 and 518 yards long, stretched out to this length because several fours are comparatively short. The seventeenth takes us downhill and across the burn we crossed outbound on number one. The round ends with a short par three returning to the recently remodeled clubhouse.

The whole experience at Kirkcaldy invites us back. The pro shop staff is helpful, and the grounds crew eager to welcome visitors and share their pride in the qualities of this fine course (one of them, Mike, brought me a brochure about Kirkcaldy on seventeen after we had talked for a moment on the fifth tee). The standard they set will color your response to other courses and clubs in Fife.

Seven in "The Meadows," part of Auld Tom Morris's original design.

23   Ladybank

The quality of a course, like beauty, may lie in the eye of the beholder. But others have endorsed Ladybank so often that you're in good company if it's one of your favorite parkland courses in Fife. This beautiful layout has hosted many tournaments and been used as an Open-qualifying course a number of times, an honor afforded sparingly. A company of fine golfers has walked these tree-bordered fairways before us. In 1978 Ian Woosnam failed to qualify at Ladybank, and in 1995 Justin Leonard's 134 made him the lowest-scoring qualifier on the course. Honorary Ladybank members Nicklaus and Ballesteros played an exhibition match here in 1983 (Ballesteros won, by the way), an endorsement in itself.

Auld Tom Morris designed the original layout with only six greens in 1879. It resembled a links pattern, with six holes played outbound and the same six greens played from the other end, for a total of twelve holes. It was expanded to nine holes in 1910, but it wasn't until 1961 that it became the eighteen-hole course we play today.

Beyond whatever interest the long history of the course may hold, those years bear particular significance today. Passing time has seen the forests mature and — more important — over time the ground cover has grown and thickened and spread so that Ladybank now leads Fife courses in heather. A beautiful purple carpet blooming in August, heather can be handsome even in the maroon-brown of its dormancy. Beautiful, or handsome . . . but also treacherous. Club manager Roy Wicks, a 35-year member here, calls the course "heather-blest" for beauty, "heather-curst" if your ball burrows into it. The back nine especially gives us fairways bounded by thick stands of tall spruce and Scotch pine, and then pinched by the club-twisting mat of steel-wool heather encroaching from both sides of the fairways to narrow them.

A warning is implied on the first tee. Patches of heather bracket the fairway fifty yards off the tee, irrelevant for now except as foreshadowing of more

Open-Qualifying Courses

LADYBANK
LEVEN
LUNDIN
SCOTSCRAIG

Even from altitude Ladybank's patches of heather stand out.

to come. After two straight holes, number three is a welcome dogleg right. Decide how much of the corner to cut. Too ambitious and you're stuck short of the fairway in a stand of silver birch and fir. Too conservative and you're through the fairway corner into heather, beautiful at a distance but as ugly as rusty Brillo pads when you're staring straight down into it, searching. The third ball I found in that heather was mine. The first two were the contributions of other golfers on other days.

There are two par fives on the front (making that nine a par 36) and only one on the back; all of them are interesting at 550, 540, and 530 yards, two of them doglegs. The par threes are equally fair (although at 243 yards, number twelve will require one-putting the green for most of us to card a par). Number eight is a tough little green, with a large bunker at the front. Off to the left in the pines lies another green under construction to replace it one day; but that won't soften the course. The current eighth may then replace the first green and be approached from the other side.

The ninth is deceptive. A tree-lined dogleg left at 401 yards, it ends in trickery for the first-time visitor here. The band of mounds crossing in front of the green is actually 75 yards short of the putting surface (though just in front of a temporary "winter green" sometimes used). The mounds aren't the problem; they conceal the problem — a deep grass bunker across the front of the green. Fly your approach all the way to the pin. The ball won't run an inch if it lands short. The second time playing the course, familiarity will make the ninth hole at Ladybank not so much an easy par as a possible par.

The back nine has more heather, more trees, and narrower fairways. And at 3,343 yards it's longer than the front but a stroke less on the card, at 35. The last five holes (three of them among the original Auld Tom six) are all par fours, the shortest one 387 yards. With thick stands of evergreens at both sides, you'll rarely see more than one other group on the course. There's little wind down between the ranks of sheltering trees, and the still fairways feel secluded.

The closing hole calls for a tee shot over a depression too small to be a valley. It's filled with birch- and whin-covered mounds, with a band of heather across the fairway at the far end of the depression, only a 90-yard carry. The clubhouse is hospitable, the snug pro shop one of the best organized and equipped you'll find in the Kingdom. Ladybank is first class from beginning to end, on the course and off. Most golfers visit Fife to play the links courses first, but Ladybank may be the best choice for those who'd like to enjoy the parkland courses equally numerous in the Kingdom.

24   LesLie

In 1998 the Leslie Golf Club celebrated its centennial with the publication of a booklet excerpting club minutes over the century. In many ways the minutes echo the experiences of other Fife clubs: an original course laid out by Auld Tom Morris, a subsequent move to another location nearer town, the fencing of some greens to keep grazing livestock from stamping cloven divots in the putting surface (it happened at Anstruther as well), admission of women members, tournaments conducted and competitions won, and so on.

Founding president Charles Anderson — the Fifer who designed and patented the hole-cutting iron — was a friend of club-maker Allan Robertson, the original "golf professional" (whose clubs Anderson played). Anderson hired Auld Tom Morris to lay out the course, donated the club's first trophy, and in many ways represented the sort of enthusiast every club needs to prosper. An article in a 1902 issue of the British magazine *Golf* termed him a "formidable player" and listed his many competitions and trophies won. He'll be remembered a long while for all his achievements.

Leslie, the course for which Anderson was responsible, lies at the base of Basillie Laws (that is, the low Basillie hills). It's bordered and on three holes bisected by a small burn, and plays to a par of 62 over its 4,940 yards, with four par fours and five threes. Two of those par fours surpass 420 yards in length; three of the par threes exceed 200. It's a short course overall, though not short hole by hole, however contradictory that sounds.

The first three holes and the ninth lie in sight of the clubhouse, while four through eight are packed into a small patch of land 200 yards away over a service road. Most confusing, the eighth green is nearly as far from the clubhouse as the property allows, requiring a walk of 400 yards or more back through the course to reach the ninth tee. The dumbbell-shaped acreage was unpromising from the start, but a redesign or even renumbering might help a course that today seems two separate layouts.

Weekenders enjoying the course at Leslie.

When I first visited Leslie, work underway (installing fairway drains?) dissuaded play. I saw only a single golfer on the nine holes in the time I spent walking the course. Since then I've been back. The burn makes two holes interesting and the turf is in good shape, but still more needs to be done if Leslie is to measure up to the other private courses of Fife.

25   Leven Links

The first tee shot at Leven easily clears Scoonie Burn, curling around the front of the tee box. One glance to the left shows that we're not done with that treacherous little stream. Scoonie Burn was historically notorious for its noxious stench. Running clear these days, thanks to regular trenching operations at the seashore to clear silt and sand from the burn mouth, it lurks unseen behind the sixteenth green and lies in wait to ambush your second shot (or third) on the eighteenth, a 448-yard difficult par four finish to one of the most enjoyable rounds you'll have in the Kingdom of Fife.

Former captain of Leven Golfing Society, David Dowie, an acquaintance by mail and a man deeply involved in Fife golfing activities, arranged a match for me with Sandy Herd, secretary of the joint committee that controls the course on behalf of the two clubs, Leven and Leven Thistle, that share play on this true links course. The proposed match gave me mental whiplash for a foolish instant: a golfer named Sandy Herd won the Open at Hoylake in 1902! How old could the man be?

This Sandy Herd's not an Open winner, but he's tough enough. He's been a scratch golfer here for 25 years and knows Leven — and Lundin next door across Mile Dyke — as few others do. In fact, he offered a description of Leven Links that distinguishes it from its counterparts nearby, even from Lundin, its "twin" beyond the dividing stonewall. On every hole at Leven, no matter how difficult it may look when you stand on the tee box, there is a bail out position, an escape. Number ten serves as a good example. It calls for a blind tee shot carrying 185-plus yards over a gorse-dotted ridge to an elevated fairway; but to the right of that ideal line lies comfort, a visible landing area stretching from 80 to 180 yards off the tee. A shot placed there could leave you with only an iron (admittedly, a blind shot) into the green of this 325-yard par four hole. Shorter hitters can play Leven, too. Straight counts for more than long.

Sandy himself is both long and straight. On number one he risked the out

The undulations of Leven Links, beyond 18 green, and Scoonie Burn.

of bounds on the right — road, car park, and beach — and crushed his drive into the narrow stretch right of the ridge that bisects the fairway, leaving himself a mid-iron into the green. I bailed out to the left side of that ridge onto the wider, safer side of the fairway and faced a 180-yard shot into the wind — for me, that day, all of a four-wood. I avoided embarrassing myself for at least one hole, and we both made par. Mine was lucky, his expected.

Although there are no hills to climb at Leven, the course is nevertheless more undulating than level, full of unexpected uneven lies and tilted stances. Unlike stateside courses created by planting groves and bulldozing tons of earth, Leven exists as the sculpting tides and winds determined centuries ago. Golfers have enjoyed play on this stretch of land since time out of memory. Rumor claims that Mary, Queen of Scots, played over these links on her way to Wemyss Castle for a tryst with Darnley, her future husband. In 1754, schoolmaster John Grubb was struck in the left leg by an errant golf ball here and eventually lost the leg. In 1846 golfers moved from the old course at Dubbieside (where history says the gutta-percha ball first entered play) a mile away. Unofficially, golfers chased a featherie over this landscape long before that.

Leven Golfing Society is the eleventh oldest golf club in the world. When the course was extended from nine to eighteen holes, in 1868, under the design direction of Auld Tom Morris, the inaugural match on the "new" course was won by Young Tom with a 36-hole score of 170 (to his father's 189). The Standard Life Amateur Champion Gold Medal is awarded to the winner of the oldest open amateur stroke-play championship in the world, played at Leven since 1870.

Even to players unconcerned with Leven's history, this links course feels traditional, from uneven footing on the sandy turf to the brilliant yellow gorse that blooms as early as March and flourishes into summer. There's the occasional sight and the constant sound of the sea bordering the east-bound first four holes, and what we'll call "the breeze" (when it's kind) or "wind" (when it's not). Swooping gulls cry constantly. It's only when you three-putt that their piping laughter seems personal.

Making the turn on nine at Leven Links.

The tee shot is blind on number two, with a pair of unseen bunkers lying beyond a shaggy ridge dead center some 205 yards out, but that's off the medal tees. From the tees we use, the bunkers are 40 yards closer and not a threat for most of us. The next two holes, both with humped fairways that tend to steer the tee shot right or left of center, take us to Mile Dyke, past which the holes now part of the neighboring Lundin course are plainly visible. Stitching the two courses together is the beachside stretch of 3 x 3 x 3 foot concrete blocks, the antitank barrier laid during World War II to thwart a feared invasion, Fife's miniature Maginot Line. The blocks are ranked down the right of Leven number four headed east, the left side of Lundin number four headed west.

We turn inland here to the deceptive number five, the first of three par threes in the next five holes. It's only 140 yards to the green, the green sloping away from the tee. Any sort of following wind can send your tee shot off the back.

After the long par-five number six, we reach the prettiest stretch of the course. It closes out the front side. The par-three number seven green lies tucked beyond a cottage-size set of gorse-covered mounds, and eight — a shortish par four at 350 yards — is worth a visit even without your clubs. To the right of the narrow fairway a steep slope reaches up to the municipal Scoonie course high above. The slope is rich with birch trees and beech, gorse in bloom into June or July, interspersed with the cream-colored blossoms of elderberry shrubs and later the wine-red berries themselves.

But admiring the foliage can divert the player from his real task: choosing the right club in the face of a misleading view down the narrow fairway ahead. Two slit bunkers cross the fairway *not* immediately in front of the green, as they first appear, but 75 yards short of the putting surface. They're in play not on your second shot but now, as you stand on the tee, debating. Lay up. The bunkers may lie 270 yards off the tee, but that's within reach when the fairway's as hard as summer sometimes bakes it. A four-wood or a long iron leaves you with a wedge or short iron to the pin. Get the tee shot right, then take time to admire the beauty of the hole.

At 3,006 yards (par 34) the front nine is a treat compared to what lies ahead. Having lulled the player into complacency, the course pounces with a back nine 3,429 yards in length, and par 37. The most interesting holes are the parallel par fives, twelve and thirteen (both 482 yards from the tips and one into the wind, the other wind-aided). Just as you're tiring, the holes grow longer: three closing par fours at 386, 414, and 457 yards.

The closing hole is in a class by itself. If your card isn't boast-worthy already, eighteen won't make it so. Members play it at 448 yards, with Scoonie Burn looping around the green and always in mind. The preface to an 1894 poem describes this water hazard as "yellow as Pactolus or black as Styx, or . . . the colour of ketchup, the density of pea soup, and with the smell of Gaol fever."

It's a threat to everyone. At the 1999 Scottish Champion of Champions tournament played at Leven, English amateur champion Mark Sanders went into the third round of the 72-hole tournament three shots out of the lead. All three lost shots came on eighteen, result of a double bogey six and a bogey five in his first two rounds. Scoonie Burn had twice reached up to snatch his ball in mid-flight and steal the tourney lead from him, or so it must have seemed. Contending for the medal, he'd had no choice but to go for the green.

Most of us will lay up. If you're one of the few who can reach the generous putting surface in two, you'll have conquered a fine hole, on a finer course. Members watching from the lounge of the handsome Victorian clubhouse overlooking the last green will nod in quiet recognition for that feat and mentally add your name to a fairly short list.

26 LOCHGELLY

Like so many other Fife courses, Lochgelly was originally nine holes. Play began here in 1904 on the 26 acres that house the front nine, and the course was extended to eighteen holes a decade later. Like other courses, Lochgelly has undergone change over the years, but unlike most others, recent changes stem from a specific event.

A neighbor's home near the fourteenth green suffered under a barrage of sliced tee shots on that par-three hole, resulting in shattered roof tiles. The neighbor threatened to sue. A compromise was reached, the hole closed, and a new hole to replace it tucked into the already snug front nine. Numbers four, five, and six used to be four and five . . . and that explains why first-timers here will find themselves turning circles looking for the right tee box early in the round.

The front nine has three threes and five fours after opening with the only five on the course. The back has seven fours and a pair of threes, for a total par of 68 over its 5,454 yards. After snarling you in the maze of holes three through six, the course settles down. It's a tight layout with all the marks of a traditional parkland course: mature plantings (being supplemented by additional landscaping underway), small greens, and several doglegs calling for well-shaped tee shots, especially when they're blind.

The first hole, named "Lang," isn't all that lang, 479 yards straightaway and a probable par to start your card. With six short holes in the modified front nine you'll reach the turn admiring that card. The turn may be unique, with a par three at number nine, another at ten, followed by six straight fours.

The par fours are made interesting with small touches. Number thirteen, "The Ditch," is only 308 yards long but isn't as easy as it sounds, because a ridge crosses the fairway diagonally left to right 200 yards out. Landed short of that, a drive kicks into rough on the right. Fly the ridge and the ball bounces left into a copse of silver firs. What's the perfect shot? I don't know.

Lochgelly, one of Fife's more "natural" courses.

Neither did club member and playing partner John McKenna, who warned me about the hole in advance. Then, playing out of the firs, he took a double bogey, too.

Number fourteen is only 336 yards long, but it's a left-to-right dogleg with tall evergreens filling the elbow of the turn. Interestingly, number fifteen, a right-to-left dogleg headed back up the hill parallel to fourteen, features three fairway bunkers placed not to catch a tee shot off fifteen but to prevent players on fourteen from cutting the corner and taking a shortcut up the adjacent fairway. Significant attention has been paid to keep golfers from dominating this relatively short layout. Good scores here are earned, not given.

It's a course that requires precision, not length. Only three holes call for a driver; all eighteen demand precise iron play. Sited atop rolling hills, Lochgelly offers fine views of rich farmland to the north and the Lochore Meadows Park across the valley. It's a hospitable place to work on your short game and course management, and you'll enjoy meeting club members. Some private clubs suffer visitors. Lochgelly welcomes them.

27   Lochore meadows

The nine-hole Lochore Meadows golf course sits atop one of the largest land reclamation projects ever undertaken in Britain. Millions of tons of fill and topsoil were trucked in to cover and level 1,200 acres of pits and mineshafts left by a played-out coal-mining operation. When visitors to this wooded parkland course compliment the park director on the lush greens, he credits the possible fertilizing effects of plentiful coal residue only a foot below the putting surfaces.

Dominating the slope leading uphill beyond the first green — in an area recently acquired for the expansion of Lochore Meadows to eighteen holes — is the towering superstructure whose pulley system once lowered miners into the now-buried shafts. A recent renovation of the structure cost £120,000. When you visit the course, whether it's still nine holes or eighteen by then, that white tower gleaming in the sun will guide you north out of Lochgelly to the village of Glencraig and the expansive Lochore Meadows Country Park.

Sited in the center of the park is the 260-acre, memorably named Loch Ore, across the road from the course. Rainbow and brown trout stock the lake, where boating, fishing, swimming, and even classes in windsurfing are available. Some in your party may head for the beach while you're across the road enjoying the course at Lochore Meadows.

Be aware, it's a low "meadow." Look for standing casual water after any sort of rain, at least until the next afternoon dries the course. The soft fairways mean little or no roll. If the card says number nine is a 429-yard par four, it plays to all of that.

A burn crosses holes one, three, eight, and nine, but you won't see it from any of those four tees. Cutting the wooded corner of the dogleg right opening hole has the side benefit of shortening the distance to that burn. A carry of 200 yards will take you past it to safety; 190 won't.

Occasional blind shots make familiarity with the layout worth three or four

Built atop recovered coal mines, Lochore Meadows is a public venue.

strokes a round on your card. At least that's the improvement I enjoyed on a second visit. No great challenge awaits us here. It's a straightforward, open course. What the proposed second nine may bring, with its hillside location, remains to be seen. The current nine's ups and downs are moderate, making it an easy course to walk. Both eight and nine have a depression crossing the fairway to create the blind shots mentioned: a blind drive on number eight, a blind approach shot on nine.

The best news is that the greens are hospitable: large, receptive, and essentially level, with good turf. Maybe there's something to the unlikely claim that coal dust in the soil has a benefit. Whatever the case, Lochore Meadows' greens give back a stroke or two lost to unfamiliarity with the course.

When you visit Lochore Meadows, slip a fly rod or spinning rod into your bag. If the greens don't reward your visit, cross the road. The day I played the course, two fishermen walked away with eight-pound rainbows. More of them swim in Loch Ore.

28 Lundin

In his *Little Red Book*, Harvey Penick advises that to improve your game, you should compete with someone. Play for a wager, however small. The challenge, pressure, and camaraderie can take your game to a higher level.

Agreed. Most golfers are sociable sorts, and a round of golf can be more memorable for the companionship (or even for the needling) than for the quality of play. But many golfers, Scots not least among them, know it's possible to enjoy the game in no company but your own.

It's a fact I saw illustrated a few years ago at Troon. Grinding my teeth at the embarrassing round I was finishing, I glanced across the stone wall toward the Portland Course next door to see a woman pleased with the prospect she faced. She looked to be about seventy, a yellow cardigan settled over her shoulders and three or four clubs cradled in the crook of her elbow. She was strolling outward bound, as my foursome headed for the clubhouse to settle accounts. Her head bobbed in time to the tune she was humming. Everyone in my harried foursome was focused on our swollen scores and the sums owed (an original bet muddled by four presses), and no one wore a smile like hers. She was there to enjoy golf: the course, the walk, and her own company.

That's how it worked out for me at Lundin, one of the two adjoining courses (the Siamese twin of Leven Links) on the edge of the wonderfully named village of Lundin Links. The course shares a boundary with Leven on the coast twenty minutes southwest of St. Andrews. I arrived about 9 A.M., hoping to work my way into a group lacking a fourth. A threesome had just teed off and the next group wasn't scheduled until 10 A.M. With the permission of club professional David Webster I set out on my own. "Follow the man in the red cap," Webster said. "He knows the way."

We were essentially a loose foursome, with one of us straggling half a hole behind the other three. All of us carried our bags. The pace was perfect. We walked the round in just over three hours, my solitary play coasting comfortably behind their three-ball. The pace allowed ample time for debating each shot: "Is this a five-iron? A six?" And it allowed me to judge where the others in my elongated foursome played their tee shots, and what line they sought for their approach toward the pin. The result was a 76, the third- or fourth-lowest score of my life and one I've never matched at Lundin, though I've been back to try. (Club captain Alan Stuart pretended to count passing clouds while I hacked my way to a 94 in his company one subsequent rain-drenched Sunday.)

So I admit that my pleasure in the Lundin course comes partly from that first experience, a success earned by playing against the course instead of worrying about the scorecard or an opponent with his eye on my wallet.

The walk itself is rewarding. The first hole, called "High," is a 424-yard par four along the high ground above the beach, with Largo Bay and the Firth of Forth to the left. Somewhere unseen beyond the morning mist drifting over the water lay Edinburgh, a gray-stone bastion only a fantasy at this distance.

Red-cap and his partners caught my attention with their tee shots, driven a full 30 degrees right onto the eighteenth fairway adjacent to number one. It didn't seem likely that all three would accidentally push a tee shot on the same hole, so I followed their obvious lead. My drive into a flat area shared by the first and eighteenth fairways left me with a longish second shot uphill into the slightly domed first green. It also in effect widened the target, just as a bowler uses the full width of the lane by aiming diagonally for the seven or ten pin down the length of the alley. That broader target meant my hooked three-iron finished left of the green but neither long enough nor left enough to find the beach. Safe and dry. A pitch and two putts earned a five. Bogey to start the round, good enough.

A par on number two, a birdie on the third — the 335-yard "Bents" — and I pawed in my bag to find a pencil. It might be a good idea to keep score.

Number four is the killer, to my mind the toughest hole on the course (no matter that the card gives it a stroke index of three): 452 yards along a broad and humped fairway, remains of a tank barrier on the left, and the sea, out-of-bounds, beyond it. More important than the length is the narrow but deep burn guarding the front of the green. Common sense suggests a layup. An uncommonly good tee shot left 210 yards to the green. No layup today. My thinned four-wood traveled about 195 yards, a line drive that cleared the burn by feet (good break number one), hit hard in the slope (break number two), and bounded onto the green to stop only fifteen feet from the stick. Two putts, a par, write it down! I made a mental note of what I'd had for breakfast. The unusual good luck had to be coming from somewhere.

The front nine, par 36, has only one three, one five, and seven fours, yet it's varied enough to be anything but boring; it's a stiff test in the onshore winds, and fun all the way. The greens are firm, making approach shots demanding. The par-three number five turns inland at Mile Dyke, at the point where the original shared course was divided in 1908 to become Leven Links to the west and Lundin to the east. Each club kept half the original eighteen-hole links course they had shared and added nine new holes inland of the original nine to create its own eighteen.

Turning back east at the sixth hole, the course parallels an abandoned railroad bed on the right. The right-of-way creates a rare mid-course out of bounds seaward of six, seven, and eight, inland of one and two. I followed the line of play Red-cap set as an example and reached the turn one over par for the front nine. One over, on a British Open qualifying course I'd never seen! Results like that might be all in a day's work for the threesome up ahead; for me they were nearly miraculous. Credit one lucky putt after another.

On number ten my attention flickered. A burst of cockiness had me smiling at the tee shots of my three "playing partners" as I watched from the ninth green. Two of them hit irons. All three laid up short of a fairway bunker that was 202 yards off the tee, according to the course planner I consulted. Only 202? I could carry that!

My tee shot plugged in the wet sand, dead center in the bunker. The threesome had been right. The six-iron I tried moved the ball three feet in the soggy bunker and illustrated what a wise man once said: a double bogey is caused by one bad shot . . . followed by two stupid shots. My hubris led to a well-deserved six on the par-four hole, which restored some humility. The rest of the way in I followed the threesome with slavish attention to their course management.

Hole number twelve, lengthened a few years ago from 133 to 150 yards, rises sharply to the green. The mounded putting surface isn't visible from the tee box. Be long, rather than short, and reach the back half. Another climb takes you to the tee box of the par-five number thirteen. It heads back west along a high flat ridge between a copse of evergreens on the right and the seacoast visible across five fairways to the left. There is a wonderful view of the Leven course dead ahead, past Mile Dyke. But coming off thirteen green

Ideal linksland, edged by golden gorse.

you'll see fourteen, the third and last par three on the course and a hole more ominous than wonderful. The tee shot is steeply downhill, into the wind. Only 175 yards away, back toward the sea, the green waits beyond several mounds and waist-to-shoulder-high gorse, whin, and bramble; it's also surrounded by half a dozen bunkers. A short hole, it will nevertheless worry anyone with good sense.

Take a moment after your tee shot to count the greens you see: Lundin is the only course I've ever visited where all eighteen greens are visible from a single spot on the course, here on the fourteenth tee. That view was the good news; there wasn't any bad. The bogey four I recorded was more than satisfying; it was a relief. (On subsequent visits I've taken a five and a lost-ball six.)

The closing three holes are once again links land. Two of them resulted in scrambling bogeys as I focused too much on the score I was beginning to hope for and pulled the tee shot on consecutive holes into the first cut of rough, ankle-deep fescue left of the fairway. The closing hole, 442 yards from the tips, played itself: a wind-aided 235-yard drive, a fading four-wood that took a carom off the sloping hillside right of the eighteenth green, found the putting surface and rolled to a stop eight feet below the flag.

When the putt dropped for a finishing birdie, the other three in my elongated foursome were already taking seats at a table inside the lounge and watching through the clubhouse window. One beckoned, a mimed invitation. The others smiled as I trudged up the hill past the window to the car park, waving my thanks. I decided not to join them. I wanted to replay the course in my mind after enjoying three hours of focused, silent golf. This is the first time I've talked about the round.

But not the course. That, I rave about often.

An occasional Open-qualifying site, Lundin measures 6,377 yards, par 71. It's a course that combines traits of links and parkland, a hundred or more bunkers, several blind tee shots, and blind approach shots, all of it made more challenging by the wind that wafts or howls off Largo Bay but seldom disappears. On this relatively calm day the course was benign, inviting me back. I enjoyed Lundin. You will too.

29 Lundin Ladies

The complex traditions surrounding three of the four contiguous courses in Lundin Links and Leven have inspired several published club histories. Let me try a brief summary. In 1908 the crowded seaside course once shared by Leven and Lundin was split at Mile Dyke under the guidance of James Braid. Nine holes on each side of that stone wall became the core of a new course, with a second parallel nine added inland of each. But crowding continued on the Lundin half because the Lundin Ladies Golf Club — established in 1891, the world's oldest separate ladies' society, now with its own clubhouse, starter, greenskeeper, etc. — also played there. Braid designed a new layout for them as well, north across the road on historic ground in the Standing Stanes Park, essentially the Lundin Ladies course we play today.

All this is straightforward enough . . . until we consider the Standing Stanes (stones) themselves, a course signature far more memorable than any signature hole. The stones — three freestanding, irregular red sandstone pillars fifteen to eighteen feet tall — stand in the second fairway. From the tee they look like a huge Roman numeral VI. Passing near them the golfer can see at close hand the crust of lime-yellow to dark-green lichens and moss on the stones. One unlikely report claims that a fourth stone stood with them in the eighteenth century but has since disappeared. They're remnants of a Bronze Age lunar observatory (like Stonehenge?), or possibly a religious site some 3,500 to 4,000 years old. Local tradition says an equal length of each stone extends straight down underground to hold each unbraced monolith erect. They remain a mystery, except to the historically naïve compilers of one guide to British golf, which confidently announces that the stones are "Roman." We'll play around them.

When it's your turn on the first tee, slip your £12 greens fee through a slot in the door of the starter's shack, just above the sign reading "Thank you for

The sandstone pillars at Lundin Ladies remain a mystery.

your honesty," and step up. At 4,730 yards, par 68 for twice around the nine holes, the course appears easy, because short. But the course record is 67.

Braid laid the course out in a pair of fields set against each other at 90 degrees, like the two strokes of the capital letter L. The first and second holes head west. A right turn leads to number three atop a distant hill. Number four parallels three back down the hill. A turn left onto five, and the rest of the nine are essentially parallel to the opening two holes.

Both scorecards — one in yards, one in meters — announce distances for general play, but the ladies' medal tees may add (or subtract) up to 50 yards from those numbers on a given hole. The opportunity to change tees and tee shots creates variety where nature and Braid's design provide little. Ninety yards forward of number five tee is a little-used tee box available to shorten the 310-yard hole to 220. Number six appears on the card at 145, but four different tee boxes offer the chance to stretch or cut that distance.

The sixth hole is the most interesting. The green is tucked behind a three-foot-high berm with a path cut through it. Immediately beyond the green,

Hatton Burn burbles past loud enough to distract the golfer hunched over a putt. And a mile away past a swath of cultivated slopes stands Largo Law, in spite of the name the highest point on the horizon and a handsome backdrop for the sixth green ("law" means "low hill").

The eighth is a par four, and number nine leads uphill toward the cottage-size clubhouse behind the final green. From the ladies' medal tees the green isn't visible. An aiming post is. The regular tees, located on a flat area thirty feet higher than Hatton Burn, give a clearer view of the closing hole.

Pleasant enough, the Lundin Ladies course might attract more play if it were elsewhere. But even located across the road from two of the most enjoyable links courses in Fife, Lundin Ladies is a very popular venue during summer vacation months.

30 pitreavie

As much fun as playing the links can be, there's a special delight in an early morning walk through the quiet aisles of a woodland course. As you strike out alone before the first scheduled group off the tee with only the birds for company, here and there a grounds crewman whipping the dew off the greens, and the damp fairways spongy underfoot, it's as if you'd stumbled upon a course misplaced in the forest.

I had that pleasure at Pitreavie, Dunfermline's (alphabetically) third eighteen-hole course. With a competition scheduled for 9:00 A.M., the starter sent me out at 8:15, after I pledged a three-hour round to keep well ahead of the members. I was on number seven and already delighted with the course when I saw the first group reach the third tee.

Pitreavie — designed in 1921 by Augusta National co-designer Alistair MacKenzie as a sports venue for Dunfermline's "working class" — tosses down the gauntlet at once. It opens with a 470-yard par four (457 from the yellows), a blind tee shot uphill, then down to a burn crossing the fairway 90 yards from the pin, and uphill again to a very small green. No birdies here, thank you. Halfway along the par-five second you see ahead the sycamore grove at the end of number three, and it's on three that the character of Pitreavie asserts itself.

Evergreens down the right, a hedge out-of-bounds on the left, the third hole is 190 yards to a dramatic two-tiered green, beyond a burn and backed by a grove of 60-foot-high sycamores. The tee boxes for four, seven, and fourteen — as well as the greens for three, six, and thirteen — all nestle into this grove. They're linked in a broad semicircle by a woodland path that leads through cool, quiet shade.

Each hole on the front nine holds a surprise, whether it's a tiered green, a blind shot, or the burn snaking across the fairway. The eighth, after a blind

Pitreavie's third green backs into a grove of tall sycamores.

tee shot, runs along a broad ridge at the highest point on the course. The view features the Firth to the south, the rooftops of Dunfermline to the north.

Number nine has both a blind tee shot and a tiered green, in addition to a 160-yard carry over a steep ravine. Clear that (and get your breath back after the steep climb up the far slope) and it's a wedge into a long, narrow sloping green that falls away from the shot.

If you pause here on the high tee to tote up your card after nine, take a thoughtful look at number ten fairway. A dogleg left, the fairway slopes to the right and crosses a burn at the green. More important, the aiming post in the middle of the fairway is seriously misleading. It doesn't take the slope into account, and a four-wood directly over the post can end up twenty or thirty yards into the right rough. Aim down the left edge and let the slope take you back to the center.

After the par-three twelfth, a string of moderate-length fours and a 200-yard three (number sixteen) lead to a strong closing pair. The seventeenth and eighteenth are par fours, 433 (452 from the medal tees) and 464 yards long. The last is a dogleg right that ends beneath the clubhouse patio where members gather, glass in hand, to watch your arrival.

With established plantings throughout, a burn on twelve holes, nicely varied fairway shapes, and challenging opening and closing holes (par fours at 457 and 464), Pitreavie asks you to use every club in your bag. On six holes I hit a four-wood off the tee. The first and last par fours called for driver, driver, short iron. Add the feeling that this course has been waiting for you, and you'll understand the pleasure of visiting Pitreavie. Try to make that visit in the early morning, or the early evening, when you may be lucky enough to have the course all to yourself, one hole at a time.

31 st. michael's

Halfway between the links complex at St. Andrews and the Scotscraig course in Tayport is the village of Leuchars, site of an R.A.F. base near the St. Michael's club and course. The pilots at Leuchars fly their approaches over the Eden Estuary and these courses. Golfers among them must smile to recognize one "secret" of St. Michael's unseen by those of us who enter the course over the narrow stone bridge leading off the highway to the clubhouse and the first tee.

Like other courses in Fife, St. Michael's has undergone a number of revisions and modifications since it first opened. In 1905 it was a nine-hole course. Since 1996 it's been a full eighteen. The back nine appears to include several holes from the original front nine. We'll reach them later.

The new opening holes of this upland course present a misleading picture. Broad fairways separated by rows of recently planted trees, with any gorse and mature shrubs mainly out of our reach at the course perimeter; ample greens; few bunkers; fewer blind shots: this is an "easy" course that looks too new to be approaching its centennial. From the third tee, high point of the course, we survey a checkerboard of farm fields and the steeples of St. Andrews in the distance.

What challenges exist on the front nine are modest and subtle. Number six is a 327-yard par four whose right-to-left sloping fairway doglegs slightly right around a large mound that hides the flag from our view on the tee. All along the left is out of bounds. Number seven is a par three, all carry across a shallow valley, and it hints at what's next. The eighth is 260 yards, 190 of them carry over a deep valley. The broad, level fairways of the first few holes imply an ease of play not present on the later holes.

Each nine contains a single par five, two threes, and six fours, but similarities end there. The fairways on the back run between large stands of mature pines, making St. Michael's an upland course on the front, parkland after

The 15th hole, a surprise late in the round.

number eleven. The fourteenth is the par five on the back nine, 480 yards long, and offers the first serious surprise. Midway down the fairway, but invisible from the tee, a deep bowl occupies the entire fairway rough-to-rough for some eighty yards. Only the longest hitter will reach it off the tee; only the shortest won't clear it with his second shot. But the real drama lies ahead.

Beyond the fourteenth green, the fifteenth tee shows us the unexpected. The fairway of fifteen drops one hundred feet or more, only to rise half that to the platform green of this par three beyond the deep pit. The card says 138 yards. It's all of that and more, all carry, and a steep decline (and then climb) to the green and the tee box for number sixteen. The sixteenth, "The Saddle," calls for two blind shots, 170 yards into a bowl high above the tee, then 150 over the bowl lip and steeply down to a green placed hard against a pond. Number seventeen requires a tee shot over that pond and blind second shot to the green high above. These three holes are out of sight from everywhere else on the course and surrounded by forest. They comprise the patch that only an aerial view — or hard-won experience — can show us. And climbing these demanding slopes you can understand why some knowledgeable members here — including the pair ahead of me and the threesome behind — played only as far as fourteen green, then backtracked along the edge of the pine forest to the tee at eighteen.

Coming off seventeen green we climb through the piney wood at least 100 yards uphill to the meadowland tee box at eighteen, and the easy final fairway down the slope to the clubhouse.

Think of the better-known championship course at Nairn, north of the Highlands, where the Walker Cup matches were played in 1999. It's similarly schizophrenic: fifteen holes of one type, three of another. A links course, so people tell us, Nairn runs along the shoreline for nine holes, then turns back on itself — a typical links layout — only to make an unexpected detour, turning right up a forested hill for three parkland holes before returning to the links.

St. Michael's is upland except for three hilly, tumbled, links-like holes that might have come off Burntisland or Kinghorn. Whether these holes make the course more interesting or only more difficult may depend on the golfer. One guarantee: your legs will remember the climb. And when you later drive past the course, like the pilots overhead, you'll recall the three hidden holes so uncharacteristic of St. Michael's.

Halfway between the neighboring villages of Saline and Steelend on highway B913, a few miles north of Dunfermline, is the nine-hole Saline course. It's spread up the western slope of Kinneddar Hill, with four holes on the northern face and four on the southern. A single hole (number three) crosses at the base of the hill perpendicular to a row of huge sycamores that once separated a pair of farm fields now united as the golf course.

The course has been here since 1912, although it did close for a time during World War I. Membership has waxed and waned. The clubhouse once burned and had to be replaced. All in all, the history of the club and this course has been uneven. Today matters seem settled, although expansion of the course to eighteen holes might inspire a spurt in membership. It seems out of the question on this hilly, constricted site.

The views here are long and varied. North across the valley is a working farm where cattle and sheep graze in pastureland surrounding a multi-acre stand of gorse. To the south, sunlight shimmering off the Firth lights the horizon, and villages dot the intervening hills and valleys. For some visitors the views may be more interesting than the course.

From the clubhouse we can see holes one, two, eight, and nine. Numbers four, five, six, and seven lie beyond the row of sycamores that splits the course. The greens we see are all of a type: small, flat, and attached to the hillside like shelves. Downhill from each flag the edge of the green is five or six feet above the sloping terrain, while the uphill edge of the green is tucked into a vertical cut in the hillside. Even some of the bunkers lie perpendicular to what skiers call the "fall line," the steepest way down the slope, rather than in any necessary relationship to the greens near them. Probably little could have been done with the unvarying slope of this site, except to lay out holes across the hill, as at Cupar, instead of up and down.

With seven fours and two threes—a nine-hole score of 34—the course

The starter's box, closed for the day.

Trolley's beside the tee.

offers more variety than a first glance promises. Holes range in length from 160 to 372 yards, with club selection a challenge because of the need to factor into your decision the steep hill that lengthens every uphill shot and shortens every downhill.

Saline fields a strong foursome for team competitions around Fife. (I watched them compete at the Fife Club Championships in Aberdour in 1999.) Five groups were playing the course the spring afternoon I visited Saline, and all were clearly enjoying themselves on their home course, despite the hill climbing that stays with me as the defining trait of the course. With three fine eighteen-hole courses less than a dozen miles away in Dunfermline, I probably wouldn't walk Saline often, even for the exercise.

33 Scoonie

Down the left side of number one at the Scoonie course in Leven runs the notorious Scoonie Burn. A poem published in 1894 said of this tiny stream, in part:

By flower and fern you roll your burn,
By links and daisied dell,
Fair fields of tilth—then why your filth,
And whence your fateful smell?

The six other stanzas are no more complimentary. Birds won't drink of it, eels and fish can't live in its polluted, stinking waters, or so it was said a century ago, when no golfer could see the murky bottom. But then, the Scoonie course didn't exist until 1911, well after the burn it incorporates had earned its reputation. Leven Ladies Golf Club managed the fifteen-hole course until 1938, when the Town Council took over its management. Today it's an eighteen-hole muni, and the burn is a clear-running stream. A hooked second shot lying in the burn (a lateral hazard) is easy enough to spot in the clear water. It still costs a stroke. Yards away, back toward the sea, the burn passes through the Leven course, where it affects far more scorecards than it does here.

John and Freddie led me around the course. Freddie, at age 79, showed the way with his 180-yard drives, unfailingly dead center in the fairway, and reminisced about other Americans he'd met: Bing Crosby, Bob Hope—celebrities, certainly, but more interesting to Freddie as golfers (one good, one not). He watched to see whether I'd measure up.

Only 4,979 yards long, par 67, the course makes for a pleasant walk and offers several enjoyable—if not very difficult—holes. Not a single par five here, there are thirteen fours on the course, only one three on the front side, four threes on the back. Several of the fours require two shots longer than

Walking at Scoonie, sharing stories the whole way.

Freddie could manage. Three of them are longer than 435 yards, and even the shortest measures 325, with the rest nearer 400 than not.

There are several blind shots and bunkers cannily placed to catch the unwary. On number four my second shot just carried the green-front sand bunker, only to disappear into a second slit invisibly tucked three feet behind the visible first bunker's raised rear lip. "Bad luck," John said. "I thought you knew about that." He took the hole, and the 10p skin, trying not to smile.

Numbers two and nine share a broad double green whose putting surface isn't visible on either approach shot — only two of the nine or ten blind shots on the course. The Firth of Forth can be seen from several vantage points in the second nine. You look south over the adjacent Leven Links to the Firth and quickly understand an anomaly. The two courses share a boundary (Leven number eight, for instance, runs alongside, but significantly below, Scoonie's seventeenth), but one is links land, the other an upland course only yards away.

The usual hazards exist at Scoonie, along with rules about a free drop away from newly planted saplings and so on. But charity isn't the rule. Balls finding their way to the "concrete surrounds at Club House" must be played or incur a penalty for a drop. Hitting your wedge or putting off the concrete driveway at the clubhouse not only saves you from a penalty stroke. It also entertains the regulars offering advice on the shot while they wait their turn on the first tee.

Inevitably overshadowed by the impressive Leven Links course next door and Lundin just down the road, the public course at Scoonie is pleasant to walk and play, even on weekends, when it may be crowded. Sharing a round with long-time members like Freddie and John, and hearing their memories of golfing in the Kingdom for more than half a century, adds to the fun.

34 SCOTSCRAIG

The Scotscraig Golf Club was founded in 1817, when it began to conduct semiannual competitions consisting of three circuits of a six-hole layout located in the midst of a racecourse. The six holes had hosted play long before the club was formed, and today the Scotscraig course retains them, three on the front nine, three on the back. Scotscraig is only a short distance from the sea, eleven miles up the coast from St. Andrews in the village of Tayport. It feels like a links course through much of the front nine, an upland course on the second nine and wherever the pine groves cast their shadows.

Whatever descriptive term is applied to the overall layout, Scotscraig must be played — even more than most courses — one shot at a time. It's long (at 6,550 yards, par 72) and narrow. That's not a combination to comfort most golfers.

Trouble awaits the opening tee shot. From the first tee we face a narrow fairway split by a ridge running diagonally left to right down the center and flanked on the right by ankle-high rough. The rough is backed by a deep ditch further right, which is backed in turn by gorse and broom in a hedge fully seven feet high, which is backed by out of bounds. Anyone who's ever sliced his first swing of the day will aim well left.

Wrong. That way lies deep, grassy rough not as dramatic as the whin on the right, but a problem as well. Hit it down the center and the shot may leak to the right 210 yards out, down a slope into rough unseen from the tee. How, then, do you play this hole? You have three choices. Either carry your drive 220 yards (neither can I), lay up at 200, or play number one prepared to hit your second shot from a tough lie.

Number two is characteristic of Scotscraig in another way not revealed in the printed course guide. In a printed diagram the hole appears flat, level, broad, and straight. Underfoot it's the most undulating, uneven, depression-pocked fairway you'll ever play . . . until you reach Scotscraig's numbers five,

Heather's beauty is a siren's call. You're better off in the bunker.

six, and seven. Bunkerlike basins and dips bite at the sides of the fairway, narrowing it until we're left with a flat central lane no more than eight paces wide at spots, ten at others. It makes the broad, flat fairway of the par-three number three a visual relief, but irrelevant. The best tee shot on three will fly to the green on this 195-yard hole without touching the fairway.

Number five is remarkable. There's scarcely a five-yard stretch of level fairway. That's not to call it "unfair": as your playing partner whose drive finds one of those small level spots will smugly remind you, we all play the same fairway.

Scotscraig is great fun because of the challenge it represents, not in spite of it. Think before each shot, then execute what you've imagined. All courses reward such a focus. Scotscraig demands it and punishes lapses, at least on the front nine.

The back nine is 200 yards longer, but the fairways are broad and more nearly level, the greens ample and receptive. A burn crosses eleven, fourteen, and fifteen but shouldn't come into play. On eleven, for example, the burn lies 360 yards off the tee on this 450-yard par four. Any problems with the burn will come from a duffed second shot. There are fewer blind shots on the second nine than on the front, fewer surprising lies, but still enough test in the length that you relax at your own risk. Between them the two nines ask you to use every club in your bag, one of the marks of a fine course. Scotscraig is that and more.

A course this old, so closely allied with the traditions of The Old Course and the membership in St. Andrews, has its own fascinating history. One record set here ought to raise a few eyebrows, of admiration or of doubt. Start by recalling what the featherie ball was like — a top hat full of boiled feathers stuffed and packed into a bullhide cover. In 1820, Scotscraig member Sam Messieux hit a featherie a measured 361 yards, 20 yards farther than F. G. Taits's then-record 341-yard drive with a gutta-percha ball.

We're in good company playing Scotscraig, where past members and visitors set a standard of play not easy to match. Even when the links courses at St. Andrews aren't too busy to welcome you, Scotscraig will reward the eleven-mile drive from the Auld Grey Toun to the north coast of Fife.

35 THORNTON

The approach to the Thornton course is misleading. A side street leads from the high street of Thornton, once the center of the Fife coal field, past a schoolhouse and between a few pairs of semidetached homes. It becomes a narrow lane pointed toward an apparent dead end against the embankment of a commuter railway line. A dark opening in the embankment is the square mouth of a small tunnel under the tracks onto a tree-lined driveway in an unexpectedly lush park. Like driving through the looking glass.

After playing a half-dozen rounds on the bunker-pocked and windswept scabby fairways of the more demanding links courses in Fife, Thornton's grassy breadth and near-flawless greens offer an especially welcome break. The clubhouse is nearly new, its bar lounge spacious and comfortable. The parkland course surrounding it is home to every native species of tree that grows in Fife: beech to birch, sycamore to oak, fruit trees, spruce and pine, conifers and deciduous alike. There's no gorse, no heather . . . and they're not missed. Golfers not yet tested to exhaustion by the most challenging courses of Fife may at first find Thornton bland, but even they will come off the course smiling.

An eighteen-hole course since 1969, Thornton opened for play at nine holes in 1921. Initially, access to the course was through a farmyard instead of under the railway, and a club rule forbade members to smoke while crossing the farmer's property. During World War II Thornton members played only six holes, the other three having been planted with crops in support of the war effort (the same was true of other Fife courses as well).

At 6,155 yards, par 70 (only one par five on each side), the course is full-grown and testing enough. More than half the fours are 400 yards or longer, though only a few holes have bunkers near enough the greens to mention. A fast-running "burn" that passes through the course is actually the river Ore.

After fighting seaside winds elsewhere, Thornton's level stance and broad fairways can be a relief.

It churns and burbles alongside four holes on the back nine loud enough to be heard even when it's unseen.

Both nines are marked by broad, straight fairways, with a good bit of to-ing and fro-ing along parallel holes. The back nine becomes more challenging as it progresses, especially with the 530-yard par-five thirteenth made difficult not by tricks of design but by ankle-deep grass rough at the verges of a crowned fairway. Number fourteen introduces us to the burn, and fifteen is a dogleg left, with a steeply canted right-to-left fairway and the burn at the base of that slope.

The sixteenth is a short, handsome hole best played with some humility on the tee. At only 244 yards, it invites the long hitter to go for it; but given the right-to-left slope and the six bunkers arrayed across the front of the green, the drive had better carry 230 yards or more. The safer tee shot is a long iron, then a wedge to a one-putt birdie, while the big hitters are flailing their way out of those bunkers.

At 291 yards with a blind tee shot, number seventeen also calls for some care. Forty yards short of the green (but unseen from the tee) a sprawling bunker fronts a ridge crossing the fairway like a fence to stop the ambitious from unleashing the driver. Once again, long iron . . . or trouble.

We arrive at eighteen tee with the sudden realization that this "easy" parkland course has just put us through the wringer with four very different holes . . . in a layout that some people will swear is all much of a muchness. And best of all, there is no course in Fife in better playing condition than Thornton. For a visiting American it's a welcome treat to hit the lob wedge off thick grassy turf into a soft green.

36 tuLLiaLLaN

In Kincardine, a river port where a bridge across the Forth handles traffic headed south toward Glasgow, is Tulliallan, the westernmost golf course in Fife, only yards from the county line. On the horizon lie the Ochil Hills, high enough to rate as small mountains in some minds. The hills central to the Tulliallan course aren't that dramatic, but they offer enough climbing to satisfy most golfers.

At 5,459 yards and par 69, the course is short but nevertheless nicely varied. One par four is only 273 yards long. Five of the dozen others are over 400 yards, including number sixteen, "Road Yett," 447 yards and the highest point on the course. It offers fine views all around: the Ochils to the west, the Firth to the south, and the checkerboard of farm fields stretching away at every hand.

After a pair of short opening holes the course turns uphill at the third, a 436-yard par four called "Sunnyside." If the length and the climb weren't challenge enough, there's a burn crossing the fairway fifty yards short of the green, as unlikely as it seems to find water running across the top of the hill rather than at the bottom. The burn comes into play on eight holes, most emphatically as a dividing line between numbers eight and nine, where it lies in wait for a faded tee shot on either hole.

The most distinctive trait of Tulliallan greets us after a blind tee shot on number five. Crossing the brow of a hill we're greeted by a fairway stretching ahead of us in dozens of regular undulations like the swells on a sea. With its evenly spaced waves — it's four paces to the top of each undulation, another four into each depression — the fairway looks like a washboard leading toward the green.

For a newcomer to Tulliallan walking these waves of turf for the first time, it's difficult not to stop short and stare. The same pattern extends left into the seventh fairway, and beyond that to ten and eleven. The geometric undula-

Setting out on the first tee.

tions appear again, crossing fourteen and the parallel fifteen, much too regular to be a natural formation. None of the three golfers I caught on the tenth tee could explain the phenomenon. If you've figured out an explanation already you're quicker than all four of us. Two other golfers we asked shrugged. "Must be for drainage," one said, but then why would they be across hilltops and not in the low fairways?

It was an eighty-year-old we met in the clubhouse after the round who explained. "Plowin'," he said. "Durin' the war. They were crop fields then."

Many of the Fife courses suspended play during World War II or became nine-hole layouts, as they sacrificed fairway space to the war effort. The space became marshalling areas for troops or equipment, gun emplacements, air warden lookout stations, or simply fields used for crops grown on the cleared land. In developing (or reclaiming) the course after the war, greenskeepers at Tulliallan simply planted grass over the fields and the patterned undulations gouged into the land by plows and cultivators.

No course in Fife better deserves the term "undulating" than Tulliallan.

The back nine, at 2,709 yards only forty yards shorter than the front, seems easier. "The Burn," number eleven, is the best birdie opportunity on the course, in spite of the fairway undulations. It's a short but handsome par four, 273 yards with a pond and forest on the right and the burn curling across in front of the green. Coming off the thirteenth green, we walk down a woodland trail to the fourteenth tee, which points uphill parallel to number three, taking us across that high burn again. The hole is 492 yards long and distinguished by two blind shots: one off the tee and — once past the burn — a second shot that may or may not reach the green. "Roundal," number fifteen, is a par three sitting high above another rippling, furrow-scored fairway, and then it's back downhill on sixteen (409 yards, but downhill enough to require only a driver and short iron) to finish the round with a pair of short fours on the flat. The last two inbound holes parallel the outbound first and second holes and take us back to the clubhouse and well-stocked pro shop.

The distinguishing trait of a course stays in memory more than whatever score you might card. If you find yourself in the west of Fife, a round on Tulliallan will show you acres of corduroy fairways and a burn that climbs hills.

afterword

By the time these comments reach print, the pair of eighteens under construction at St. Andrews Bay (probably to be called "Kingask" by Fifers) both may be open. Another course, Forrester Park in Cairneyhill only a mile or so from the Dunfermline Club at Pitferrane, certainly will. A nine-hole public course at Cluny Clays is promised; another at Dunino is rumored.

Perhaps most interesting of all, a "new" James Braid course is in the works. It was home to Dunfermline until 1929, when the club moved to the Stutts-designed layout at Pitferrane. The Braid course near Torrieburn remains nearly intact, and a local group has approached the County Council — so some say — seeking permission to reopen. We may yet see a new James Braid course, in the twenty-first century!

All these rumors and promises of more courses to play invite yet another visit to the Kingdom. They certainly suggest the good health of this ageless game, but for me any new courses in Fife will belong on the other side of a line that events have drawn across the history of golf in the Kingdom.

At 3:40 P.M. on a July Friday in 2000, Jack Nicklaus finished his second round at the Millennium Open in St. Andrews, unfortunately missing the cut. There's seldom if ever been so great an ovation as the one he received, and deserved, walking up eighteen. Most fans in that crowd recognized that Nicklaus probably won't play in the Open over the Old Course when it returns here in 2005. They said goodbye when they cheered the man, his career, and the traditions he created as well as those he has honored.

After his final putt he walked toward the R&A clubhouse and the number one tee box, where Tiger Woods was ready to tee off at 3:50. The two shook hands, exchanged words. Nicklaus passed through the crowd at the tee, and Tiger went to work. It was, for many of us watching, the end of one era and the beginning of another, marked by this public laying on of hands. The event marked a new millennium, a new championship to be won, and a new champion to win it.

When I returned to St. Andrews the following year, I once again played several of the less familiar courses "hidden" in the Kingdom. One was the Jubilee. For the first time, I played it with hickories, replicas of Auld Tom Morris's clubs, on a course he designed. For me, golf in Fife will continue to mean those courses in play before and into the year 2000. Other golfers will enjoy the newer courses as they become available. I hope, however, that they also sample the existing layouts and discover for themselves all the courses in the Kingdom. There's real delight in the discovery.

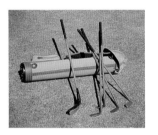

index

Note: Page numbers and Fife courses noted in **bold** indicate primary discussions. Photographs are shown by *f* (for *figure*).

Give the gift of
aLL the courses in the kingdom
to your friends and playing partners

_____ YES, I want ____ copies of aLL the courses in the kingdom
(isbn 0-9726308-7-2) for $39.95 each.

_____ YES, I'd like to receive advance notice of Richard E. Peck's forthcoming novels.

_____ YES, I'd like to be added to the mailing list for REPertory Publishing.

_____ My check or money order for $_____ is enclosed.
Make check payable to REPertory.

Please charge my ___ Visa or ___ Mastercard.

NAME _____

ORGANIZATION _____

ADDRESS _____

CITY / STATE / ZIP _____

PHONE _____

EMAIL _____

CARD NUMBER _____

EXPIRATION DATE _____

SIGNATURE _____

Include $3.95 shipping and handling for one book, plus $1.95 for each additional book sent to a North American address. New Mexico residents must include 6% GRT. Canadian orders must include payment in US funds, with 7% GST added.

European orders require payment in us dollars, $9.00 shipping and handling for the first book, $4.95 for each additional book.

Payment must accompany orders. Please allow three weeks for delivery.

SEND COMPLETED FORM TO

REPertory
Post Office Box 1278, Placitas NM 87043

OR CALL
877-REPertory
(877-737-3786)
www.REPertory.com / FAX 505-771-1009